EVEN IF

STACY MEHAFFEY

aBM

Published by:

A Book's Mind

PO Box 272847

Fort Collins, CO 80527

Copyright © 2020

ISBN: 978-1-953284-28-0

Printed in the United States of America

I dedicate this book to those who are
hurting, hopeless, disappointed and devastated.
May you find the hope, strength and courage
to take the steps that will secure your destiny
and positively impact your future.

Even If…

TABLE OF CONTENTS

ACKNOWLEDGMENTS

When I first began writing my story down on paper, I had no idea what its purpose would be. Would it be a diary for my children to someday read, was it a form of therapy to strengthen my weakened mind or was it for something more? I didn't dare dream it would one day be published. When you think of all the influences on your life's story, everyone in it has impacted the outcome; because I firmly believe that everyone is intentionally placed in your life for a reason. I would like to take a minute to thank some of the standouts.

First, I would like to thank my husband Chip. You have been my strength, my rock, my comedic relief and my biggest fan. Thank you for believing in me and for making me believe in love again. I love you!

My dad. You have always been the most amazing example of a father. Because of you, I learned the delicate art of a well-told story. You have also taught me to work hard and to believe that I can do anything I put my mind to. Thank you for loving me no matter what.

My mother. You always had high expectations and taught me to never give less than my best. You taught me through example how to be strong. You gave me my sense of humor and a childhood full of memories that make me smile. Thank you for giving me a safe and loving home to grow up in. I love you.

My sister, Tonya. You have been the most amazing example of strength and grace through tough times, not allowing your pain to be wasted but, instead, to be used to directly impact my life.

My brother, Jeff. As my first childhood friend, you shaped my life. You ensured that those early years of my life were filled with grand adventures.

Monty, my firstborn son. I think you may have taught me more than any other person on this earth. You taught me about unconditional love and that God doesn't expect perfection, only a heart that believes. You taught me to believe in miracles and for that, I will forever be grateful.

Chad, my child who is the most like me. Thank you for your undying love and compassion for a mother who at times let you down. Thank you for your support and encouragement to make this book happen.

Whitney, my daughter, my mini-me. Thank you for not just being my daughter but for being my friend. Without you, I would have never been able to complete my degree and build a better life for our family. Thank you for being the first to encourage me to write things down as a therapeutic way to begin healing.

Mackenzie, my daughter not by birth, but by choice. Thank you for accepting me as a parent in your life and for helping develop my storytelling abilities by always requesting to hear just one more of my stories.

My friends. For years I felt so alone but each of you have fulfilled a very specific purpose in my life. Each of you held me up when I was unable to stand on my own. Stephanie Powell, you showed me that someone can make it through a tough time and still come out beautiful. You also showed me that my story can strengthen others. Deedee Mast, you showed me the importance of being a friend even when you are dealing with your own stuff. Tracy Talley, you will always be my very best friend forever and ever and your support over the years has been invaluable. Pam Hall, thank you for being that friend that needs no filter. Thank you for praying me through the panic attacks and for loving me through it all. I don't know what I would have done without any of you.

ACKNOWLEDGMENTS

JR Moffatt, thank you for giving me that very first safe opportunity to share my story publicly and for giving me the confidence that my story could make a difference for people who were going through tough times of their own.

Robin Wood, thank you for kick starting this journey, first by writing your encouraging book of miracles and second by reaffirming that my story was worth telling.

My publisher, Jon McHatton, thank you for reigniting my passion for telling this story and believing in my ability to make it happen.

My editor, Misti Miller, thank you for helping me organize all my thoughts and for putting them in a format that others could read and understand.

Most importantly I want to thank you God for hanging in there with me and loving me when I probably wasn't being all that easy to love. Thank you for bringing me through all the tough times. Thank you for loving me enough to write every page of my story. *Even if...*

INTRODUCTION

You must appear perfect. You must never let your deficiencies show. You must never air your dirty laundry. You must never be late. You must never be soiled. Appearances are everything.

These are the voices I hear in my head daily. While driving me to attain that never attainable end goal of perfection, these voices also paralyzed me. They made me feel isolated and alone because if I ever let anyone know the true me, they surely wouldn't like me. I was flawed. I was a screw-up and I had been for years. The weight of hiding the true me was crushing.

If I could only find one other person who was flawed like me, maybe they would be agreeable to befriending the real me. The problem was, there seemed to be no one like me. Everyone else seemed to have it all together. Everyone else had the picture-perfect marriage with kids who behaved and respected their parents. Everyone else had the money for everything they needed with extra left over for their many indulgences.

So, the farce which was my life continued. No one could ever know my imperfections. They were more than imperfections; they were bombs that I had exploded in my life. Explosions that by my own doing, had destroyed any hope of making something of myself. I once had so much potential. How had I ended up here? I grew up in a loving home with supportive parents and never lacked the basic necessities of life. I went to sleep every night in my own bed, with my blanket, in my room in our house with my parents fervently watching over me from their bedroom at the bottom of the stairs. Every morning I had plentiful options to fill my stomach which was never hungry, and my day continued with endless play only intruded upon by the occasional uninvited chore bestowed upon me by my ever-present parents. I pretended to be annoyed by them but, in reality, they made me feel like I was part of something. I was important to my family. My family appeared perfect and it was not until I was grown that I realized there is no such thing as a perfect family. Even when doing what you believe is best, we all make mistakes.

Sometimes in life I have felt alone. I learned early on that you don't get everything you want, but my parents always made sure I had everything I needed. I never felt hungry or in danger. After leaving the safety of my childhood home, all that changed. For years, I had prayed to God to fix my situation yet here I was, still stuck right in the middle of it. Finally, out of exasperation, I felt as though the only saving was going to come through doing it myself. I became self-sufficient, still believing in God, but losing faith that He would do anything to affect the circumstances of my life. I wrestled with the thought that a good father wouldn't fix my mess and make my path easy. My path has been anything but easy.

Life had set me up perfectly and I had gone and messed everything up. One foolish decision followed up by another and another had now left me as far from that perfect childhood as one could be. I didn't know what else to do but to continue to protect my secret. So long as no one knows what is really going on, maybe they will at least believe the illusion that I am worthwhile.

It was not until that façade was shattered that I began to understand the power of being real. You see, when you speak your terrible secret something amazing happens. It loses the ability to control you. You take back your life. Although bringing my secrets out into the light was by far the scariest thing I have ever done, it was also the most empowering. I found out that not only will people look past those imperfections, they also will be drawn to you, not despite them but because of them. This went against everything I had ever believed and was astonishing to me. Maybe, just maybe, I could be the person for others that I so longed to find, when I was buried in the rubble that had become my life. Because of this, I have decided to tell my story. This is a real story about the real me, the one I have been hiding for most of my life. My hope is that by being real, I can help others see that perfection is nothing but a well-kept secret. We all are less than perfect, and I will no longer be held prisoner by my imperfections. Even if it won't be easy, I am taking back my life.

I felt ill-equipped to face the life I found myself in, but God had seen to it that I had exactly what I needed. He knew I required a loving father who loved unconditionally, made me feel as though there was nothing I couldn't do and to dream big. Also vital to my equipping was a demanding, no-nonsense mother who expected greatness from me and taught me to give nothing but my best, even to all whom God placed directly in my path. This ultimately gave me another one of the many tools I would need to overcome what I would someday face.

As I look back over the events of my life, some amazingly miraculous and some devastatingly tragic, I can see how they are woven together for my good. I love the analogy of our lives being like a tapestry, with all the broken strings and the mess. But they are being woven to form a beautiful masterpiece. Yes, He could have fixed my situation, but I became stronger coming through it and everything that happens is not about me. I don't know all of the whys; I don't have all of the answers, and I likely never will know some of them this side of heaven. I would love for God to give me a life free of pain and to deliver me out of all my trouble, but even if He doesn't, still I will trust him.

Even If...

1

PERFECT CHILDHOOD

To say it was an easier, simpler time would be, at best, a colossal understatement. An old Southern Gospel style hymn had just come to an end and my mother was swiftly walking back from her place at the piano. The sound that resonated from that quaint small-town Baptist church was quite magnificent as my dad's deep voice perfectly blended with that of his five brothers, two sisters and the multitude of other relatives that had all piled faithfully into the church that early Sunday morning. As we settled in on a cold, hard-backed, creaking pew, in our unspoken assigned seats, the second row from the back near the window, I was nestled on my daddy's lap with my head resting on his strong chest and his solid arms wrapped lovingly around me. I am quite certain he believed I was drifting off to sleep because I was sitting so still, but as the preacher droned on in the background I was intently listening to the steady beating of my father's heart. The rhythmically entrancing sound was indelibly relaxing. I tried to sync my breathing with his leisurely deep breaths but try as I might I could not match it. I wondered how he was able to breathe so slow and if I could ever be like him. My daddy was my world. Imagine, if you will, the safest, most delightfully cozy easy chair ever created. That is the privileged position that comes to mind when I fondly reminisce about my very earliest memory in life.

I was born into a conventional Christian middle-class family in the antiquated town of Losantville, Indiana, population 200, give or take a few. The inconsequential town was nothing fancy, but it had the necessities including a bank, post office, grocery store, gas station and one flashing stoplight. I came into the world a full month early weighing only 5 lbs. 8 oz with a head full of platinum blonde hair. I wholeheartedly believe I had my daddy wrapped around my little finger from the moment he laid his beautiful blue eyes on me. If the opposite is possible, he had me wrapped around his finger too. I loved my daddy more than anything. I suppose one could contend that he was a zealous workaholic, but I preferred to see him as an adept provider. He worked at the GM plant in Muncie, Indiana from the time he was 19 years old. For most of my life, he worked second shift and left for work at the insanely early hour of 2 p.m. and did not arrive back home until around midnight, long after I was sleeping soundly in my bed. In my opinion, this was entirely too long for any doting daddy to be kept away from his adoring daughter and I abhorred his time away. Many an afternoon I heard him yell "bye" followed by the distressing slam of the back door. This invariably sent me frantically running through the house in absolute fear of him slipping away without one last hug, only to find him contentedly standing by the door with the world's biggest smile of gratification on his face. All my fears and worries instantaneously vanished as I flew into his steadfastly awaiting arms with my heart beating wildly as my little world was slowly set right once again.

My dad and me playing with a puppy he brought home. My love of animals started early.

We lived in a moderate, white farmhouse on the edge of town just across the train tracks. My parents had bought the house from my grandpa, who lived beyond the cornfield that butted up to our garden. I believe he lived his life according to Proverbs 10:4, "Idle hands make one poor." I never remember seeing him not working. He would show up nearly every morning before the sun was up, to work around our little makeshift farm doing any chore he could find that needed to be done. I suppose it wasn't a real farm, but we had cows, chickens, barn cats, dogs, a garden and a tractor so it seemed like a farm to me. My limited world was so thoroughly sheltered. Everyone in my life was good and kind and formed a protective hedge around my little world. My mother was a stay at home mom, who was a bit of a perfectionist. Our house was always spotless, and we were expected to stringently uphold her lofty standards. I have an older sister who fits quite well into my mother's perfectionistic mold. Me? Not so much. She was the perfect little girly girl and my mother delighted in her. She delicately flitted around the house in her little ruffle dresses, painted nails and curled hair, asking my mom if there was anything she could help with in the kitchen. Ugh, the kitchen, that is the last place I wanted to be. I was a stark contrast to my sister with my dirty face, disheveled hair, bare feet and ripped blue jeans. If I had to be in the kitchen, it would be over in the corner where my mom had constructed the very best art center ever. Well maybe not ever, but to a five-year-old it certainly seemed like it was. It was full of coloring books and crayons and I would retreat to that corner to sit despondently every day when my dad left for work. With the large white oversized door open wide behind my back I would quickly get lost in my own little world experimenting with colors. I remember discovering that I could make the picture look different if I outlined each figure pressing hard, then colored the inside of it lightly. I could also get a cool effect by pressing soundly with the crayon and then using my little fingernail to scratch over the surface to make it smooth. Once my dad had left for work, I would sit for hours creating my special effects artwork. When evening arrived and it was time for bed, I would climb the stairs to the bedroom I shared with my older sister and wait for my mother to come and read us a story. I loved this time of day. She would pull out one of our many books and often personalize it by substituting our names for the names of the children in the story. This was great fun and, thus, began my love of reading. I could listen to those stories over and over and often knew them by heart. One book had characters named Winkin', Blinkin' and Nod and it had a shiny moon mirror on the front of it. Another of my favorites was about a couple of squirrels. I loved looking at the drawings and imagined I was peering into the secret life of those squirrels. Story-time was one of my favorite times with my mother and I loved snuggling in close, all of us in one bed so we could see the pictures. After the story she would go down-stairs and begin practicing her songs for the following Sunday's church service and I would be lulled to sleep by the peaceful, sleep evoking sound of my mother playing the piano.

My sister, mother, baby brother and me all dressed up and ready to go to church.

My sister was 3 years older than me and as a child I never felt connected to her. Perhaps it was because she was everything I never could be in my mother's eyes, or perhaps we were just complete opposites. She wanted to play Barbies, paint my fingernails and curl my hair. This was pure torture for me. I wanted to get outside where there were fluffy baby kittens to be found, rambling fields with arrowheads to explore, mud pies to be made, slimy baby tadpoles to be caught and tall trees to be climbed. Besides all those fun things, outside is where you could usually find my dad and anything with my dad was at the top of the list of my favorite things. I loved working around our small farm with him, pulling weeds, mowing the yard and feeding the cows. Sometimes I would get to climb up in his big pickup truck and we would go hunting or fishing. I always felt that my mother was a bit disappointed in me. I was not her idea of what a little girl should be. At times I would try to please her and help in the kitchen, but she had no faith in me. She always gave my sister the skilled jobs like making the cornbread and would ask me to put ice in the glasses. It insulted me that she thought I was so inept that all I was capable of doing were the menial jobs. So, rather than face her low opinion of me, I avoided the kitchen whenever possible. Even if I couldn't be mommy's little darling, I could still be daddy's little girl. Due to the immense jealousy I had for my faultless sister, I delighted in pushing her buttons. She was so much fun to torment. I would chase her around the house with a slithering little snake I had captured as her shrill shrieks filled the country air or purposefully don my shirt backward or wrong side out just to hear her yell out in exasperation, "You have your shirt on wrong again!" After glancing toward my father with my best wide-eyed pitiful look of feigned innocence, I would slowly turn to her to get my reward. She never failed to give me the desired response and the look of absolute abhorrence on her face was priceless as I quietly mouthed, so that only she could see, "I know." Yes, life was good until the unthinkable happened. My little brother came along. Now daddy had a real boy. I was just a substitute and abruptly found myself being pushed out. I was the middle child with no real place. I didn't fit with my mom, and my dad, who had always been my buddy, now had a real boy... Why couldn't I have been a boy? Then my position would have been secure. Having a brother wasn't entirely bad though. Even if he was replacing me, at least now I had someone who wanted to do fun things. He would play ball and explore outside with me. We quickly became fast friends.

This is me outside which is where I was always the happiest.

Sundays were the best. I would wake up early to the smell of Sunday dinner cooking in the oven and Phipps Gospel Sing playing old-time Southern Gospel songs softly on the radio. After church, Dad would often ask if I wanted to go for a ride. We would travel down an old country road called the Dalton Pike to a little country store and buy a bag of assorted candies. It was nothing fancy, just the fun of the game my daddy made it. When we arrived back home, my brother, sister and I would sit on the floor in front of him as he dumped the bag out in front of us. We then would take turns picking which piece we wanted. If you messed up and picked the piece Daddy wanted, he would loudly make a buzzer sound with his throat. I jumped every time even though I knew it was coming. You see, I would intention-ally try to pick out the kind he wanted in order to elicit the buzzer. In the end, you wound up with a pile of candy to enjoy, but that wasn't the real prize. The real prize was my dad's attention. I loved spending time with him, and Sunday was the only day he didn't work. Sunday evenings were filled with more church, piggyback rides around the living room floor and a party. The parties varied. Sometimes they were a ring bologna, Velveeta cheese and Ritz cracker party and others were my dad's secret recipe chocolate shake. My dad could make anything a party.

I don't think I was a particularly clumsy child, but my childhood did have its share of injuries. The first, of which I can recall, happened when I was in kindergarten. My sister Tonya and I were playing at our cousins' house one warm summer afternoon. Tonya was a good friend with our cousin, Lori, who was close in age to her. That left me to play with my older cousin, Greg. This suited me just fine as he was more fun anyway. He was pushing me on the swing, and I loved the feel of the wind blowing through my long blond hair as I implored him to go higher and higher. Sometimes he would run under me as he pushed the swing and my stomach would travel up to my throat as I squealed with delight. As I began to tire, I asked him to stop and he laughed robustly and pushed me even higher. When I felt my fingers slipping off the cold metal chain of the swing, I begged him to stop before I fell, but before I knew it, I was flying through the air and landing with a thud on the hard ground. An excruciating pain went through my left arm and I lay there in a heap on the ground. My cousin quickly ran to me, scooped me up in his arms and took me inside where our mothers were drinking coffee and catching up on the week's news. After a trip to the emergency room and some x-rays it was discovered that I had broken my arm. They wrapped it all up and strapped it in close to my body in mummy-like fashion. Even if it hurt, it was kind of nice to be the focus of everyone's attention for a while.

I must have liked it a little too much because I decided to do it again the next year. Well, it didn't happen quite the same way. We were on the gym bleachers waiting expectantly for the first-grade teacher to blow her whistle to signal that we could go play. It was our middle recess and was raining cats and dogs outside so that meant recess in the gym. Since recess was always the best time of the day, we were all anxiously sitting on the edge of our seats eager for it to begin. As the whistle blew and I cautiously stepped out into the row of stairs and reached for the railing, one particularly rambunctious little boy with no regard for my safety, bulldozed past me knocking me forward and I tumbled over and over as I plummeted down the gymnasium stairs. I felt that old familiar pain shoot through my right arm. I groaned with the knowledge of what I had just done and at the thought of another trip to the emergency room. Surprisingly, the school nurse, Nurse Hill, AKA Broom

Hilda, did not share my opinion concerning the assessment of the situation. You see, Nurse Hill was known for spotting attempted manipulation by children under her charge. Think you can go home because you wet your pants? Think again. She had the most hideous, ill-fitting, fowl smelling clothing awaiting you in a brown paper bag in her closet. Size did not matter. Think you could go home because you had a headache? Not happening. That would only get you a drink of water and a 10-minute nap on her mat then back to class you went. Claiming you puked? If she didn't see it, it didn't happen. So, if I thought I was going to pull one over on her and tell her that my arm was broken, I had another thing coming. She was much too astute to fall for that. She assessed my arm and promptly sent me back to class telling me to suck it up. As I sat through the next 3½ hours of school quietly sobbing in my seat, I grew to despise this sorry excuse for a nurse. She had no reason to mistrust me. I didn't lie. I always did my best to do what I was supposed to do. I wondered how long I would hurt this badly and if my mother would believe me when I got home. As I walked in the door my mother instantly noticed something was wrong. She came to me, knelt in front of me and asked me what happened. I felt my fears vanishing as I was again within the safety net of my loving family. I should have known I could trust my mom. She was always there for me. She was home every day when I got there, with a snack or an ear to listen. I burst into tears, this time not from pain but relief. From the relief of knowing I was safe and taken care of. My mother promptly drove me back to the emergency room where it was discovered that I had indeed, broken my other arm. This time they put it in a cast. This made me the happiest of all. It was like my trophy that I would proudly wear to show that evil Nurse Hill that she was wrong, and I had won.

I grew up in the days where carefree children could roam and explore and never had to worry about a creeper lying in wait to steal them away. I wandered the vast expanse of our property searching for critters and arrowheads. I was an archeologist searching for the telltale signs of a forgotten species, or an explorer conquering the rainforest discovering new creatures not yet observed. I played with the varmints and let them go. The other non-living treasures I found, I stashed in a small rectangular wooden suitcase with a little lamb on the front. This was my treasure chest. When I would tire of that, I would expand my explorations to the railroad track beside my house. I would pretend to be a private eye searching for clues in my latest case and, at times, would leave a penny on the train tracks for the next train to squash. Eventually, I would make my way uptown to the little store. I often would drag along my little red wagon, filling it with discarded pop bottles that had been flung out the windows of the passing cars. How could people be so wasteful and how could I be so lucky? I could get five cents apiece out of these and by the time I reached the store would have a wagon full. I would exchange the bottles for money and then go on a shopping spree with my earnings. If I were fortunate to have found enough bottles, I would buy a Coke in a glass bottle and a can of Vienna sausages. I would then sit on the curb in front of the store and have my little picnic. Life was good.

Although my sister and I shared very little in common, there was one day a week that was always fun. That was grocery day. Every Thursday morning, we would go into town to do the grocery shopping. It was Mom's day out with her girls, and it was always fun for us and ended in a headache for our mother. I don't know why it produced a headache for her as we did our own thing and didn't bother her.

Ok, so maybe the time she came out of the grocery store to find me holding onto my brother's feet sticking out of a trashcan, with my sister and me instructing him to fish for treasure, maybe that was stress inducing.

For the most part, though, we were little angels. This was the one day a week we got to eat out. We didn't get to choose what we wanted. It was always the same: a cheeseburger, small fries and small coke. But it was delightful. We then would walk freely around the shopping plaza feeling quite grown up as I checked every phone booth for left behind change and scoured the sidewalks and discarded carts for misfortunate shoppers forgotten treasures. On one glorious day, I put a penny into the bubblegum machine and it spewed all of its contents into my little plastic shopping bag. What luck? I got all that gum for one penny. My excitement was quickly quelled when, upon returning home and showing my stash to my mother, she informed me that if I didn't pay for it then it was stealing. I hadn't thought of it that way. We carefully counted every piece and returned the next week to pay for what I had taken. I am not sure why I was such a scavenger. Mother would always give us a dollar and we would walk down to Hook's Drug Store to see what we could get with it while she shopped for groceries. Candy was inexpensive and we found that we could get quite a lot. If chosen wisely, one could end up with a whole sack full of goodies to take home. As soon as the grocery shopping ended, we began our imploring to stop by Anna's house on the way home. Anna was my dad's sister and the best aunt ever. More often than not, my mother would concede with the stern warning that when she decided it was time to leave, we must comply without argument. It was a nice idea, however it never worked. We loved Anna and it was always too soon to leave her house. Anna was so full of love that you thought she might just explode. She would hug you and kiss you and bless your little heart until you were so full of love you could hardly stand it. She also had a candy drawer that she insisted you visit the moment you walked through her door. I don't remember what was in that drawer but the mere fact that it existed was an attestation to Anna's greatness.

I got to see Anna every Sunday at church and I would often sit right beside her with my best church friend, Jennifer, and my best cousin Becky. We would look at her many pictures of all the children that loved her, make chains out of the gum wrappers she had in her purse and eat the strange tasting coffee candy she kept on hand. After church we never wanted our time together to end and felt that we must continue the fun at one or the other's house. I would go ask my daddy first and he would tell me to go ask my mother. My mother would then promptly defer the request back to my father. I don't know why they played this little game, perhaps to build the suspense but the answer was always the same and Jennifer and I, or Becky and I, got to spend a lazy Sunday afternoon together more times than not. The best thing about going to Becky's was the ride home. Her dad took the roller coaster road home and he knew just how to use the accelerator on that 1970 station wagon, pressing hard as we sped up each hill making our stomachs land in our throats on the way back down to earth, as we squealed with delight. Becky was my cousin, the daughter of one of my dad's brothers, and she had four older brothers. When at her house we kind of just stayed out of the way in her room playing with her poodle or her bunny. One of her brothers had his own space up in the attic of her house where he housed his very own Cockatoo. I wished my brother were that cool. When I wasn't at Becky's, I was at Jennifer's. Her house was great fun. She had a pony named Sugar. We would make her a pie out of all of the things ponies love, play chase with her German Shepherd, Sugar Bear, and usually wind up in their camper playing house. We often made Jell-O™, which we drank warm because we didn't have the patience to let it gel, and added food coloring to our water, pretending we were drinking wine. Jennifer and I talked about everything and were perhaps feeling a little too comfortable one fateful day when we decided it would be a good idea to try our hands at streaking. We were old enough to know better but too young to care or to reason out in our minds what could happen. We stripped down to our birthday suits and cautiously exited the camper. The plan was to run around the camper one time and then return safely inside. No one else would even know we had done such an exciting and brave thing. What we didn't plan on was that as we rounded the final turn that her father would be pulling up the drive with a look of surprise on his face. We simultaneously bolted for the 18-inch door that was only made for one person to enter through at a time and got wedged in tight as neither was willing to let the other be first to hide inside, giving her shocked father an even longer view of our naked buns. We quickly got dressed and waited for what seemed like forever for her dad to come reprimand us, but he never came. I think he must have been as traumatized as we were. I told myself that just maybe he hadn't seen us but, as I found out upon returning home, that was only wishful thinking.

From early on in my life, I had a special love of animals. Every unwanted animal had a home with me as I dragged around huge barn cats and captured every scurrying creature that was unfortunate enough to be slower than I on a particular day. I am not sure if my parents tired more of my incessant begging or of my dragging home every stray I found, habitually claiming they followed me home. One glorious day my dad announced that we were going on a trip to the pound. The excitement welled up inside of me until I thought I would burst. The seven-mile trip to the local pound seemed to take an eternity, but we finally arrived at the steely cold prison for the county's most unwanted. As we walked into the modest white cement brick building, the putrid smell of unattended waste wafted through the air to my tiny nostrils. I was taken aback by the overwhelming smell and I attempted to breathe only through my mouth as we ventured further into the sanitarium of slaughter. I soon forgot about the stench as the wailing of the innocent, crying out for a pardon from their undeserved death sentence, engulfed my thoughts. I yearned to take them all with me as their wistful eyes stared into mine. My heart was heavy for the elder and the unattractive tail wagers. Who would ever come to their rescue? I had to put those thoughts out of my sympathetic seven-year-old mind. We couldn't free them all and difficult as it may be, I had to select just one. That's when I caught sight of a minuscule blonde figure huddling timidly over in the corner of one of the prison cells. He was trembling with fear as his tiny tail twitched ever so slightly. Who could ever have thrown this wee treasure away I wondered? Perceiving my entrancement with this pint-sized pup, my dad motioned for the guard to open the door. I tentatively reached toward the quivering pup and was met by a teeny pink tongue on my hand. I giggled as I instantaneously fell in love with my new best friend. He snuggled into my lap on the trip back home and intermittently thanked me with more kisses on my nose and face. Every kiss was met with a giggle and I speculated that I must indeed be the luckiest little girl in the world. I named the little collie mix Jay Jay, and we were instantly inseparable.

2

LIFE'S A JUNGLE

Even though I would have preferred to stay home and play outside with Jay Jay, apparently there is a law that said I must attend school. When school started up my second-grade year, I was blessed with the most loving, grandmotherly type teacher. This would clearly be a good year. Every Wednesday after school my mother played the piano for a meeting I attended in the school's choir room called, "Good News Club." One afternoon, the leader was telling us about how sin creates a barrier between God and me. That certainly was not good news! I didn't like the sound of that. I didn't want to ever be separated from God! After the meeting, I went and told her so. She explained to me that Jesus died on the cross to make a way for that barrier to be broken and that all I had to do was accept Jesus as my savior, then there would be nothing standing between God and me anymore. What a relief. I would now be able to talk to God anytime I wanted and would live in heaven with Him someday. Life was grand. I had no worries and no fears. It was as if I was living in a little protective bubble where no harm could come to me. Most of the time, I didn't really think of God after that day. He was like an insurance policy that I kept in my pocket for when I got in a bind. Whenever trouble reared its ugly head, I would give Him a call and everything would be repaired pronto. Along with this new insurance policy, however, came a heavy burden. I now felt I had to be perfect. I am sure that somewhere along the line, I had been told that I needed to try not to sin, and when I messed up and did something wrong, I needed to ask God for forgiveness. My mind heard if I messed up and then died before asking for forgiveness I would live forever in hell. I remember being scared of God. He was like the principal of a school, standing in the hallway, peeking through the doorway of the classroom of life and waiting to catch me messing up and, pow, I would be punished. I often prayed for forgiveness and wondered how many times He would keep on forgiving me. I sure seemed to mess up a lot.

Then I entered the 3rd grade. The three teachers for the third grade were notoriously evil. Our choices were mean, meaner and meanest. As fate would have it, I got the meanest one. On that first day of school, I was scared to death. I reasoned in my mind that if I did what I was supposed to do, maybe I could sail through the year undetected. After all, I was a rule follower by nature. I liked to make people happy. I thought, maybe, Mrs. Green was probably only mean if you made her mad. Yeah right! Mrs. Green did not discriminate. She was mean to good and bad alike. She may have been even meaner to those who tried to be good, at least that is what it felt like to me. It didn't matter how good you tried to be, Mrs. Green would find some way to torment you. Everyone has a birthday, right? Well on your birthday you got a birthday spanking, with the board. She had a list of everyone's birthdays and when that usually celebratory day arrived, she would call you up in front of the class, have you bend over and grab your ankles and she would count aloud as she whacked you. Let me tell you, for a teacher she sure didn't know how to count very well because inevitably she would lose count and begin again so she could prolong the torture. Why, oh why, could I not have been born in the summer? I would have to be sure to convince my mom to let me wear pants this year on my birthday. How mortifying for those who forgot and wore a dress on their birthday. Everyone in the class would see their underwear. Very early on in the year, we were separated into reading groups according to our skill. I was reading with the top readers, so I was put in a group with the other elite five. We were asked to come up with a name for our group and we decided on "Super Friends" after the Saturday morning cartoon. Mrs. Green told me to write our name on the blackboard for everyone to see. I was shaking as I fumbled for the broken piece of white chalk that was nestled amongst the chalk dust in one of the small grooves of the ledge. I reached up as high as I could and began writing. I felt my chest tighten as I struggled to remember how to spell super. Why could I not remember? That had to be a spelling word from the first grade and I always got 100% on my spelling tests. I held my breath and began to write. Then it happened, the opportunity Mrs. Green had been waiting for since that first day of school. I messed up. I neatly wrote the name Supper Friends on the board as the name of our group. In what seemed to me like her most wicked, witchy voice she crackled her taunts at me and laughed her loud wicked witchy laugh. "I thought you were supposed to be smart. Do you want to be called the Supper Friends? I can't believe you don't even know how to spell the five-letter word super." The taunting continued the rest of that day and for the weeks to come. Every time it came into her mind, she would begin her harassment again saying things like, "I would ask Stacy how to spell this word but it has more than 3 letters so she probably wouldn't know." I was mortified. How could I be so stupid? She was right, I didn't deserve to be in the top reading group. Oh, how I wished I could just disappear, and she could find one of the other terror-stricken students to oppress. After several weeks, she did forget about my innocent mistake and moved on, but her words lingered on and played over and over in my head like a recording, with the result of destroying my self-esteem. As hard as I tried to be the perfect little girl that year, it seemed she could easily find something to pick on me about. I was petrified of her threat to "tie a rubber band to my chair to flip me in the butt" every time I forgot to push my chair in. I wasn't even allowed to say the word butt and here she was threatening me by using that word. I developed anxiety issues and had daily stomach aches. I pleaded with my mom to let me stay home from school daily but to no avail. She made me go anyway. One day Mrs. Green caught me trying to retrieve my pencil that had rolled to the back of my desk. She alleged that I was laying my head down on my desk, which was strictly forbidden. My punishment was to stand up and hold my desk chair above my head until further notice. When I was in third grade, I was of very slight build, maybe 40 pounds, and very little of that was muscle. I stood there obediently holding the chair up and my scrawny little arms began to tremble and cramp. I dared not let the chair fall. I could only imagine what the punishment for that would be. Luckily, she tired quickly of this activity thanks to another kid that needed her attention. One day we had been prepared the worst lunch in the history of school lunches. It consisted of sloppy joes, lima beans and lemon pudding. I knew that the only thing I would be able to eat on that entire plate was the lemon pudding so I, along with most of my friends, bought a chocolate milkshake. When lunch was inedible, we would get a shake to fill us up. As we lined both sides of the lunchroom table with our trays full of slop and our milkshakes sitting alongside, Mrs. Green appeared at the head of the table, standing with her hands on her hips and her chin thrust toward the ceiling casting an intimidating shadow over us all. She had a new edict she was preparing to announce. Starting at this very moment, there would be a new rule. Anyone who purchased a milkshake must clean up his or her plate. We all sat in stunned silence. The reason we bought the milkshake was that we knew we would be unable to stomach the nauseating nutriment. Unfortunately, I had already wolfed down the only edible item on my plate, the lemon pudding and was left with the mystery meat sloppy joes and the vile lima beans. After approximately 30 minutes of suppressing the urge to hurl and attempting to ingest the inedible, it was finally time to leave the lunchroom and go to recess. I quickly picked up my tray and headed for the trashcan. Maybe she wouldn't see that I was unable to fulfill my obligation. I was almost home free when I felt the cold steely hand of the repugnant witch grip my arm. "What do you think you are doing?" she snarled. "You will be taking your tray back to the classroom to finish your lunch." As I slowly shuffled my way back to the classroom, my mind was racing to figure a way out of this. I had tried my best to do what I was told. My system was rejecting all attempts to swallow these substances. Every time I put a bite in my mouth it was met with violent gagging and watering eyes. I had watered it down using my milk and milkshake and had tricked my system into accepting about 1/3 of the spread and was left with nothing to dilute the abhorrent remains. We were at an impasse. As Mrs. Green stared at me with her merciless eyes and I stared at my plate with despondency, the situation seemed hopeless. Startled by the screech of wood on the tile floor from the teacher's chair legs, I glanced up to see Mrs. Green standing behind her desk. I sank lower in my chair. This was it. She was tired of toying with me and was coming over to shove the food down my throat. As tears formed in my eyes, she announced that she had to go to the office and expected that my plate would be empty when she returned. Then she was gone. I was alone in the room. I quickly glanced around the room to survey my options. The only plan that seemed feasible was to stuff the remaining sloppy joe and lima beans into my empty milk carton. I knew if I were caught, that I would be eating it out of the carton, but it seemed worth the risk. I mustered up every ounce of courage I could find and swiftly concealed the remnants in the tiny container. I closed it up tightly and prayed that she wouldn't detect my scheme. When she returned, she smiled victoriously as she surveyed my plate. She motioned me toward the door and my heart pounded as I whisked past her to the cafeteria door. I dumped my tray in the trashcan and realized I had done it. I had beaten the unbeatable and nefarious Mrs. Green. Even if her actions intended to make me think I was dumb, I had outsmarted her.

Although the effects of Mrs. Green's incessant bullying would remain present in my subconscious for the rest of my life, I survived that traumatizing third grade year. As I entered the fourth grade, I was relieved to find that this year I had the most coveted teacher in the entire elementary school, Mrs. Baker. She was gentle and kind and just what I needed to give my haggard self-confidence a boost. As if I were not lucky enough to have her for my teacher, our class got the bonus of the hottest student teacher I had ever seen in all of my nine years of life. His name was Mr. Anderson and he would become my first crush. He was so kind and so cute. I could hardly wait to get to school and the weekends passed by way too slowly. I thrived under the guidance and instruction of this top-notch team. The year went much too fast and soon it was spring, my favorite time of the year. Spring was the time when all the flowers and baby animals began appearing, both of which make me extremely happy. I had begun taking piano lessons and always looked forward to riding the bus with my sister to our teacher's house for our lessons. I would complete my 30-minute lesson and then spend the next 30 minutes, while my sister completed her lesson, playing with our teacher's Great Dane, Francis. She was a fawn color and gargantuan of a dog who stood about 4 feet tall. My sister wanted nothing to do with her. She was always afraid of dogs and found them to be a bit smelly and repulsive, but I never did. There was not much I loved more than dogs. This week was extra special because Francis had just given birth to puppies and I could hardly finish my lesson for needing to see them. Finally, my 30 minutes were over and I scampered off to the barn to meet my new friends. As I approached the big white barn, I noticed that the paint had begun to peel from the structure, and I could hear the low grunting and snorting of the hogs that were housed there. The smell of the fresh hay and the hogs blended in the breeze and it wafted to my nose, only intensifying my excitement of what lay inside. As I rounded the corner into the barn, past the sliding door that was left open just enough to accommodate a large mama dog or a small 4th grader, I spotted her. Francis lay curled around eight squeaking newborn pups. I started down the corridor toward their hideaway, back in a mound of hay and Francis rose to greet me. I reached toward her to caress her head as I had done so many times before and, in an instant, I felt a sharp pain shoot through my little hand and up my arm. Before I could process what was happening, I was laying on my back in the hay with 140 pounds of ferocious protective mama dog standing on my chest and snarling in my face. I wondered if she would kill me as I lay frozen in fear. I attempted to yell out for help, but no sound would come from my throat. The hogs in the pen alongside us squealed loudly in response to the commotion that was disrupting their afternoon meal. Over and over I tried to call out, but nothing would come. Francis' weight on my chest was crushing and time stood still as I awaited the next strike. I silently prayed for God to help me and instantaneously, the farmer appeared behind me. He scooped me up and before I knew it, we were in route to the emergency room with a towel wrapped around my hand. My parents were called and met us at the ER. As the nurse unwrapped the blood-soaked towel from my right hand, I was able to examine the damage. Half of my little finger was missing, and what remained was a gaping hole with tendons and tissue protruding out. I was in shock but curiously felt no pain. It was almost as if I were watching this happen to someone else. The surgeon was called in and there was a decision to make. The end of my finger had been found in the barn and we were asked if we would like him to attempt to reattach it. I had known a couple of people who had this type of procedure done, only to have a worthless appendage hindering their endeavors and I did not want that. I would rather have a fully functional half of a finger than to have a useless full one in my way. The decision was made to simply close the wound and not to reattach. The hospital staff told me I could have one person in the operating room with me and let me choose who it would be. Without pause, I chose my daddy. He was the strongest person I knew, and I wanted him to hold my hand. As he fought back the tears, nausea and horror, he never let me see it. He was my rock and I was not afraid with him by my side. I later learned that after we had returned home and I was safely asleep in my bed, he broke down sobbing, mourning the damaged child he loved so much. It never really hurt so much physically but it did emotionally. I worried, "would I still be able to play the piano?" and nervously inquired of my mother as to which hand the wedding ring was worn. A few malicious boys from my class found pleasure in taunting me mercilessly and would follow me to the bus chanting, "little finger, little finger," as I tried to make myself disappear under my coat. I quickly became an expert with how I held my hand. If you put your mind to it, you can always have your pinky finger concealed in some manner. I learned to discreetly tuck it under my palm or position my hand so that my clothing hid that finger and, soon enough, those loathsome boys forgot about my inadequacy, and me, and moved on to their next victim. Funny, how even after my tormenters had stopped saying those words out loud, they played over and over in my mind as though they had never stopped. Whoever said, "sticks and stones may break my bones, but words will never harm me" was sadly mistaken. I found that physical wounds heal much quicker than emotional wounds.

As if all of this weren't enough, I found myself losing my fondness for my best friend of four years. I had always been best buds in school with a girl named Katie. We spent the night at each other's house and were always together. She was a very sought-after friend. She seemed to have it all, shiny black hair, big brown eyes, flawless olive skin and a beautiful smile with perfect sparkling white teeth. And if that were not enough, she always wore the latest fashions. I distinctly remember the first time I went over to her house. Her room was the room of a princess. She had beautiful décor, a canopy over her full-sized bed and a closet that you could walk into. The walls of her closet were lined with clothes, many still had the tag on them. Around the entire floor of her closet sat 100 pairs of shoes neatly lined up, side by side. I had always wanted a canopy bed but never got one. Katie didn't even have to share a room with her sister. I was a bit jealous. I always wanted a room like that but since my sister and I shared, and she was the one in good with our mom, guess who got to call the shots? We didn't have full-size canopy beds like her. We had little twin beds that you could potentially roll out of if having a particularly scary dream, and our bedding was covered with ruffles and little lavender flowers because purple was my sister's favorite color. Purple made me want to puke. I hated any-thing girly. Why couldn't I have just been born a boy? If I were a boy, I wouldn't have to share a room with my annoying sister and my dad would still want to spend all his time with me. Katie and I had become close in the first grade, but personality differences drove us apart. Due to differences in how each of us interacted with others, I found myself distancing myself from her and feeling even more alone. As my fourth-grade year ended, for the first time in my educational endeavors, I was relieved to be away from my classmates. Even though most were compassionate and kind regarding my recent disfigurement, the damaging words of a few echoed relentlessly in my head. I longed for the carefree days of roaming the fields, with my faithful companion, Jay Jay. He was always there waiting for me and accepted each day's adventure with eager anticipation. Jay Jay was the perfect friend. He always loved me and if he noticed that half of my finger was missing, he never even mentioned it. Jay Jay taught me about unconditional love. He would stare deep into my eyes with his big brown ones and listen patiently when I was down and needed to talk. He also would celebrate with an excited wagging of his tail and a few sharp barks when I was happy. That summer we spent the days together, exploring the world around my home where I could be anything I could imagine and forget about my imperfection. I threw myself into playing imaginary games outside to quiet the voices. I was a clever jewel thief, scaling the haymow in the top of our barn, attempting to avoid the laser beam alarm system and acquire the precious exorbitant jewels before being detected. I was a courageous zookeeper fearlessly capturing enormous hairy black widow spiders, delightfully adorable furry baby moles and fierce miniature tiger cubs with razor-sharp teeth for my zoo. I was a relentless explorer vigorously slashing my way through a rain forest with a machete to discover an unidentified elusive new species of insects. But being an imaginative adventurer came at a cost. Mad killer bees and fierce ill-tempered hornets stung me to the extent that I began having nightmares about them. One night, in particular, I dreamed that they were chasing me, and I was frantically running for my life to the river just a few feet ahead. There I could escape their wrath by submerging myself in the cool water and they would be drowned. My little legs and feet, however, were no match for the velocity with which these winged assailants flew and, in an instant, they encapsulated my little body, injecting their poison with such force that the pain was excruciatingly unbearable. I threw myself to the ground in a desperate attempt to roll and remove the assailants from my burning flesh and was abruptly awakened as I fell from my bed to the cold hard floor. I began spending less time outside and more time locked in my upstairs room. It was not as much fun as exploring but it was considerably safer. I began fulfilling my adventuresome spirit through reading. With the right book, I could go places that I had never even heard about and my latest paperback could inevitably be found under my mattress where it could be easily retrieved. One day, my dad returned home from an auction with a box full of the most interesting items I had seen in quite some time. He carried the box up to my room where I lay reading a book on my bed, completely entranced in my latest adventure. It was always fun getting a surprise and I enthusiastically examined my new treasures. Dad had brought me a drawing pad, charcoal pencil set, complete with a stomp and eraser, and a book entitled, "Learn How to Draw." Maybe my dad did still care about me. He had obviously noticed that I liked to draw and possibly that I had retreated to my room. I would show him I was worthy of this gift. I would become the best artist ever. Reading books temporarily took a back burner to my renewed passion for art. I learned not only how to draw a picture, but I learned how to shade the sides of an object to make them appear to pop out of the page. I also learned how to smudge with the stomp to smooth out the edges. I read that book page by page, over and over that summer as my love for creating my first masterpieces grew zealously.

Being a preteen was a trying time as I struggled to figure out my place amongst my peers. Everyone was beginning to divide up into cliques and the most popular girls would be invited to all of the parties. Luckily, I found myself well-liked and included, except for the parties held by one girl, Pam. I honestly have no clue why she decided that she didn't like me, but the feeling soon became mutual as time after time I was excluded from every party she ever had. We became archrivals and I detested her. She was a mean girl, and I had no place in my heart for mean girls. We would glare at each other across the room and she would loudly taunt me and say hurtful things to our friends about me. As my fifth-grade year began I noticed a particularly enthusiastic little girl named Tracy in my class. Tracy was amazing. She didn't ever say anything bad about anyone. She was fun, laughed at my stupid jokes and knew about my accident the year before but still wanted to be my friend. The decision was an easy one. Katie was out and Tracy was my new best friend. We became inseparable. We spent oh so many weekends dancing on her bed and singing loudly into hairbrushes while the radio blared out the latest tunes. We would explore outside together and get into mischief from time to time but her love was unfailing. I finally knew what a best friend should really be, and things were starting to return to normalcy. I slowly drifted back into the carefree state that comes with naiveté of being 10 years old and of living in a sheltered environment. I didn't know how blessed I was to have both a mother and a father in my life. There was no turmoil in my household. My mother was always there when I got home from school. We went to church every time the doors were open, and I lived in a home filled with love. I never once heard my parents speak an unkind word to one other. My life was one of innocence and blissful ignorance of the evil that lurked just outside of the barricade of love that my parents afforded me. One sunny afternoon as I exited the bus and bounded up the driveway, I saw my dad sitting on the tailgate of his truck. What a perfect ending to a wondrous day at school. I would get to hang out with my favorite person of all times. But something was wrong. He wouldn't look at me. Well, surely it was nothing a hug from his favorite daughter wouldn't fix. I ran to him and threw my arms around his neck and he hugged me extra tenderly. Confused, I stepped back a step and saw a tear forming in his eye. As I searched his face for an answer, he slowly began to speak. Jay Jay had been hit by a train. By nature, Jay Jay was a herding dog. He loved to chase things. Birds, cats, cows and if there were no creatures to chase, he had even been known to chase airplanes. He had become a common source of entertainment for the train conductor, whose route took him past our house on a regular basis because Jay Jay would run along our fencerow as if he were racing the train. When he heard that whistleblowing, he would position himself at the edge of our yard by the railroad crossing and run the entire length of our property as hard as he could. We could hear the conductor bellow, "Come on Shep!", as the train barreled by. But on this fateful day, Jay Jay had somehow ended up on the other side of our fence and was running right alongside the train when a metal bar that was protruding from one of the cars caught him right in the head. My dad had witnessed the entire event un-fold. With tears beginning to appear in my eyes, I told my dad, "That's not funny!" but it wasn't a joke. Jay Jay wasn't dead, but he was in bad shape. The vet had sent him home saying there was nothing he could do, and he was laying in our garage on the cold cement floor. I ran to him and lay his fractured head in my lap. Maybe he would make it, I reasoned. He didn't look that different. There was a small dent on the right side near the top of his head. He looked up at me with those trusting eyes and I knew he was hurt bad. The end of his tail curled up in an attempted wag as he tried to thank me for being there. He softly whimpered as he tried to tell me he was hurting but I told him it was ok. He didn't need to talk only rest. My parents tried to get me to come in and eat supper, but nothing would tear me from my little bud-dy's side. As nightfall arrived and my mother realized I would be sleeping in the garage she thoughtfully brought out my sleeping bag and a pillow so maybe I would at least sleep. There was no sleeping that night for me as I sat through seizure after seizure feeling so helpless and inefficient as a nurse. By morning his suffering was over. The vet had been right and the damage to his brain was more than he could overcome. My best buddy was gone. Who would I now confide in? Who would love me more than anything? I was surrounded by family and friends who all loved me, but who didn't understand or accept me as Jay Jay did. I was always enough for him but now I was alone.

I don't remember much about the rest of that school year and, although I would never forget my first best friend, the sadness did lessen. As my parents wearied of my moping around, they wisely decided maybe it was time for a new puppy. We went to a local farmer's house where his border collie had a fine brood of puppies. I approached the mama cautiously just in case she saw me as a threat to her young family, but my fears were unwarranted. She was as calm and friendly as she could be. Their father, on the other hand, had to be locked up because, as they explained, he thought it was his job to protect the property. He was an Australian Shephard and they tend to be very protective. When the farmer opened the door to the barn the frolicking pups all scampered out. There were ten little black and white puppies with white tips on their tails. I imagined this must be what heaven is like as I sat on the ground and they all descended upon me, tails wagging and little puppy tongues licking my face. Oh, how would I ever choose just one? I wanted them all. I knew I had better not press my luck and began to scour the group for that special one and then I spotted him. One particularly pretty, little pup who was born with only half a tail. He was flawed just like me. We had an instant connection, as I knew he would love me and not judge my imperfection. I named him Macho, after the popular song of the time "Macho Man" and because of the way he strutted around as if his little four-pound body owned the place. We didn't do anything special but were just content getting to know each other and then that all changed. My grandpa invited my mom and me to go to the county 4-H dog show. This would be fun! I never knew there was such a thing. I had seen the beautiful dogs prance around the ring with their owners all decked out in their finest dress clothes on TV and was expecting such a spectacle at the fair, but that was not what I saw at all. At the fair, there were kids my age that had taught their dogs how to sit, stay, walk on a leash, fetch and some even knew hand signals. The little wheels in my head began turning wildly, as I imagined Macho and me doing that. He loved me so much; he would do anything I asked. I could hardly wait to get home to him to begin our training. Macho took to my novice training like a duck to water. Whatever it takes to make a show dog, he had it. He so wanted to please me, and, in no time, he had learned to sit on command. We then went to "down" and then "stay" and, before you knew it, he had a whole slew of tricks he could do. We were together every waking moment when I wasn't in school or at church. He understood people talk so much and we became so in tune with each other that I could ask him to do something and without even showing him what I meant he could do it. Not only could he do everything the first-year dogs had done at the fair, but he could also do everything the older, seasoned dogs could do as well, including heeling off-leash, standing for examination with a cat rubbing up against him as a distraction, fetching a dumbbell, staying when I left his sight, he even learned hand signals. The first-year 4-H requirements were quite a step down for his skills but we both thoroughly loved it and excelled. I looked forward to those Monday evening meetings, in hopes that the leaders could teach me more about training him, but in all honesty, he already knew it all. He stuck to me like glue, his eyes never leaving me.

PAGE 12

FAIR'S FIRST CHAMPS — The first champion of the Randolph county 4-H fair was Stacey Price (left), Union Blue Ribbon club, with her mix breed dog Macho, the grand champion of the dog show. Reserve grand champion went to Ward Lucky Leaf 4-H club member Angie Clevenger (right) and her mix breed, Tillie. Stacey is the daughter of Mr. and Mrs. Bill Price, Losantville, and showed in the first year class. Angie is the daughter of Mr. and Mrs. Max Clevenger, Ridgeville, and showed in the second year class. (Star Photo by Mary Catharine Barrett)

Me and Macho after winning the 4-H fair competition.

He wanted to please me more than anything. He was a pro. Our sessions at home would often draw a crowd, as cars would line up in front of our house to watch him do his tricks. He would jump through hoops, retrieve a coke out of a cooler for me when I got thirsty, and even hike his leg on a tree on command. When I shot my finger gun at him, he would fall over and feign death, he would show me his teeth in counterfeit anger, walk backward and crawl. I was so proud of him and so proud of myself, after all, I was the trainer. The more time we spent together the stronger our bond became, and he turned from just my friend, into my protector. I was so proud when one of the neighborhood boys began bullying me, Macho's protective instinct would kick in and he would bravely threaten to tear them limb from limb. He could be quite intimidating when he became riled. As time went on, he became more and more protective of me, but he never would cross the line and bite anyone, only threaten. We won nearly every dog show we entered that summer, even taking grand champion away from the five and six-year dogs. We were quite the team, Macho and me, and finally, I was the best at something.

Finding my way in life was a struggle through my preteen years. I was by nature a pleaser. I wanted everyone to like me and to be happy with me and it seemed to me I was failing miserably. I felt more pressure than ever to make my parents happy as my teenage sister was beginning to act out. I hated when she and my mother would argue. Many times, I sought refuge in my room when they would begin battling and would bury my head under my pillow to drown out the ghastly racket. I detested discontent and my sister was bringing it into our ordinarily tranquil home. Even though I tried extra hard to make my mother happy, I felt as though I never could. She was a perfectionist, and it can be quite a challenge to maintain perfection. I remember proudly coming home with all A's on my report card only to have my self-satisfaction crushed as she inquired why there was a minus beside one of those A's. The other girls at school weren't happy with my report card either. I learned very early on to lie about my grades to avoid jealousy. When asked what I got, on report card day, I would hide my card and say something vague like, "I'd rather not say." They would smile and proudly show me their grade cards with A's, B's and C's and they would like me because they thought that meant they were at least smarter than me. With my straight A report card safely hidden away,

I would marvel at how lucky they were to have done so well. There was one girl who I could share with. She daringly showed me her grades one day and they were all A's. From then on, I couldn't wait to find Judy at the end of a grading period so I would have someone to brag to that would be happy for me and not jealous. It was difficult juggling people. Trying to be someone they liked. For a time, I became a chameleon. Changing the me I presented to those around me in a futile attempt to be liked. Why would anyone like me? It seemed my mother wished I was different. I felt as though I wasn't who she wanted me to be. I despised anything girly, pink or homemaker like. She often chided me that she felt sorry for my future husband because I would be clueless as to how to cook or clean. Seriously? How hard could that be I wondered? If you can read a cookbook and follow directions, I think you can master that one. Besides, maybe I didn't want to be Susie Homemaker. I also seemed to always say the wrong things. I remember being shamed mercilessly at lunch one afternoon, right in front of my sister's boyfriend for referring to a cute boy as a stud. I meant no sexual connotation when using it. I thought it meant he was really handsome, not that he would be great to use to produce offspring. When she was finished, I vowed to watch my words more closely and began speaking only after close examination of the words that were about to come out of my mouth. Another time, after hearing the schoolyard boys yell out in pain and promptly clutch their nether regions, I innocently inquired of my mother as to what "balls" were. I had no clue what I had just done but the look on her face told me it was unacceptable to speak of such things. After stammering around, with her face the color of crimson I had never quite seen before, she absconded off using immense words that I had never heard before, let alone could understand. It was something about testicles and scrotum and sperm and all I learned that day was that if I had questions about boys, they were not to be spoken aloud. Even if I felt I could not live up to the lofty expectation of perfection from my mother, I had my two best friends who loved me no matter what, Tracy and Macho. Perhaps that would be enough.

Then there was this boy. His name was David and he was dreamy. He had taken a fancy to me as well and we became an item when he asked me to "go" with him. We weren't physically going anywhere but we were going together so I was on cloud nine. We would sit together at lunch and even held hands in class during a world war 2 movie. I have no idea what the movie was about because I was too busy trying to slow my heart so it wouldn't beat right out of my chest. On my birthday that year, he bought me a necklace with an emblem of a little boy kissing a little girl on it. That immediately made my heart begin to race again. Did that mean he was thinking of kissing me? I never got to find out the answer to that question because my mother got a call one day that he and his father had been killed when their small private plane crashed. I didn't understand. Kids my age didn't die. How could this be? It seemed so unfair. He was so young.

But life is not fair, and this is a lesson that would be painfully repeated that year. What started out as all fun and games would turn into a nightmare. Australian shepherd dogs can be extremely protective by nature and as Macho and I spent more and more time together, his desire to protect me grew. I utterly adored him for the way he loved me. If my dad were play wrestling with me, Macho would bare his teeth and offer a low growl as a warning not to get too rough. If my sister made me cry, he would send her scrambling up to the top of the swing set to escape his snarling teeth. If a neighborhood boy began taunting me, all it took was a low "sic 'em" from me and he would chase them flat out flying from my yard. I saw one terrorized troublemaker sprint across the yard and vault the fence in a single bound. Suddenly, no one messed with me for fear of the ensuing wrath of my savage guardian. Then one day, Macho crossed that invisible line and sunk those snarling teeth into a young boy's leg. Little did I know this would be the beginning of the end. Macho's fury raged out of control. Soon anyone who dared set foot onto our property was risking an attack. After several unsolicited bites, my dad informed me that Macho would have to be put down. He couldn't have a dog that attacked everyone who came around. So that was that. There would be no discussion. Macho was promptly taken to the vet and euthanized. As I sat alone in my bed trying to wrap my brain around what just happened, my heart mourned for my lost friend. The guilt engulfed me. This was all my fault. I had ignorantly encouraged his aggression, taking it as a display of his great love for me. I should have done things differently. Before he had become so obsessively protective of me, he had listened intently to my commands. I could have, should have, taught him to control himself. I had failed my friend, and, because of me, he was dead. Dead for loving and protecting me.

I seemed to be failing at a lot of things in those days. This was also the summer in which I got my one and only spanking from my father. I am not sure why I had done what I did but all summer long I was drug along to my little brother's tee-ball practice. It was in a lazy little town called Carlos and the only saving grace that kept me from insanity via boredom was Angie. Her brother played on the team as well and she was at every practice. We would hang out on the bleachers talking about everything under the sun and she told me about the local store. It seemed it was owned by a blind man, who couldn't see to safely secure the money he received and would often drop it onto the floor. When you went into this store, there would be free money lying around everywhere. I eagerly accompanied her to the store, and, to my astonishment, her assertions were true. The floor was riddled with coins. There was free money just laying around for bored children to pick up. We quietly picked up all that our little pockets would hold and ran from the store all the way back to the ball diamond. My little heart pounded out of my chest. What a rush. I felt giddy. I couldn't believe we had gotten away with it, or so I thought. Turns out that the adage, "your sins will always find you out," was true. My dad somehow found out and for the first time in my life took me out behind the woodshed. All that was hurt was my pride and my heart. I had disappointed my father and that hurt most of all. He then drove me back to the store to make amends for the wrong I had done. I walked slowly back into the store and tried to think of what I could possibly say to this blind man about why I had stolen his money, but no words would come. When I entered the store there was once again money all over the floor and I relaxed a little when I remembered that he couldn't even see me. I stood there for a few minutes pondering how I should go about resolving my transgression and finally decided on the cowardly way out. I threw the money back onto the floor and ran out. I am certain that this was not the apology and amends that my father had spoken of, but he never knew.

Eventually I got a new puppy, but that bond was never quite the same as the one between Macho and me. Maybe it was because I was growing older and had less time to spend with him, or maybe I was now too afraid to have him fully devoted to me, but regardless of the cause, this new pup Sabin was less than stellar when it came to training. He was not the brightest bulb on the tree and training became a chore. I had to work harder with him than I ever did with Macho and once in the show ring, he would forget everything he had been taught. He would stand up when he was supposed to be staying and when he got nervous, he had a propensity for disgracefully relieving himself right in the middle of the ring. It was clear we would never win any championships. Defecating during your exercise was an automatic 20-point deduction. With 100 points being the max, this act would quickly take you out of the competition. Poor Sabin, he was all beauty and no brains. I still loved him, but my priority these days shifted to my human friend, Tracy. Our days were filled with laughter, inside jokes and easy-going fun. I loved spending the night at her house. We would make pizza, choreograph dances to all the latest songs, go pretend shopping at the local store and talk about boys. Tracy was the only one, besides my dogs, who had that unconditional love for me. I could tell her anything and she loved me just the same. We began signing our notes to one another YVBFFEAE, that stood for Your Very Best Friend for Ever and Ever. She was even there for me on the night of my very first real kiss. I had been kissed before. Lane kissed me behind the bookshelf in the kindergarten classroom, but I am not talking about a peck. I am talking about a real kiss. The assault occurred during a middle school basketball game at a rival school. This school was loaded. I am not talking about skilled basketball players. I am referring to the hot young boys it contained. One of them had taken an interest in me and it was very exciting to have a cute boy from a school other than mine who liked me. We were sitting together during the game and he wanted to hold my hand. Butterflies fluttered in my stomach as I felt a new feeling that I had never experienced before. At halftime, we went out to the concession stand to get refreshments. When the buzzer sounded signaling to return to our seats he seemed to be lingering. Being a rule follower, this bothered me, but I pushed the urge aside to do what I was supposed to because he was so dreamy. He offered to show me where his locker was. I readily complied. Who cared about the lame basketball game? I had Jeff asking to hold my hand and give me a tour of his school. As I excitedly took it all in, he suddenly stopped. I reasoned he was getting ready to point out his locker. Boy did I ever read that wrong. Before I knew it, he had come in for a kiss. Oh well why not, I reasoned. I pursed my lips in preparation and then it happened. This dreamy boy's lips touched mine. My heart soared as the room began spinning and my spirits were floating up in the clouds. Then I crashed back down to reality in an instant. What just happened? Did he really just stick his tongue in my mouth? That was nauseating. His tongue came into my mouth and touched my tongue. Why would he do such a disgusting thing? Did other people do such acts? I ran to the bathroom and vigorously washed out my mouth. Once Tracy and I were back at her house for the evening, I revealed the violation to her. She agreed that it was quite an unfortunate incident and that it was thoroughly repulsive. We fell asleep giggling and sharing our deepest thoughts and dreams and our utter disgust for this new revelation about what boys liked to do with their tongues.

3

TEENAGE DEFIANCE

As I entered the preteen years, I began thinking more and more about boys. I had always gotten a lot of attention from them, likely due to my blonde hair. I had questions about things. Was it ok when they wanted to hold my hand? What about if they want to put their hand on my leg? How about a tongue in my mouth? What was sex? How did babies get here? After the fiasco that resulted from my one and only sex question a couple of years earlier, I knew that asking my mother was not the route I wanted to take, so I asked my sister. She told me that she had heard that to get a baby you take a pill and then nine months later...presto, you have a baby. I asked my friends and they told me something about a big bird that drops the baby off at your house. I may not have been the smartest preteen ever, but these explanations just didn't seem plausible to me. Surprisingly enough, I discovered that the school library was a plethora of knowledge. You could find magazines that told it all and my friends who shared my love of books had begun reading romance novels. I became obsessed with making sure I understood sex so that one day, when I got married, I would make my husband happy and would not be embarrassed about anything. I did an extensive self-study and found out all kinds of interesting things and my sister and my friends were definitely not correct with their explanations. In my quest for knowledge, I asked my church camp counselor the question that was weighing heavily on my mind. Where was the line? What was ok to do with boys? I didn't want to make God mad at me and I didn't want to do anything wrong and according to the magazines and books I had been reading there was a lot more to be done than just kissing. My church camp counselor was about as helpful as the other adults in my life. His answer was, "Heavy petting is ok." What? I didn't have a clue what heavy petting was and now that I am a parent and I know what it is I don't think that was probably the best answer he could have given me. The adults in my life were failing miserably at this sex education thing but it seemed ok because I still had my books to learn from.

Near the end of my 8th grade year, to prepare us for the transition to high school, the entire class got to take a tour of the school we would be attending. High school seemed so scary and so big. I tried to make a mental note of where each classroom was and what hall went where and then we entered the art room. As we walked around the room there was a class in session. Toward the back of the room I saw something that stopped me in my tracks. There was a girl drawing a picture. Not just a sketch, like I could do, this was an actual life like picture. She had sketched an underlying picture and was about halfway down the page with filling in the details. I watched as her masterpiece unfolded, mesmerized. I never knew one could do such things with a pencil. It was incredible. I could hardly wait to be in high school so I could take this class and learn to draw like that. As Tracy and I prepared to begin the exciting transition into high school, another tragic event hit my life. Tracy's parents announced that they would be moving away over the summer. They were going to Colorado. I was terrified. How would I do this high school thing without my BFF? We pleaded with them to change their minds but to no avail. The decision had been made. They would leave and she would enroll in school there leaving me to begin high school here alone. The tears wouldn't stop, and immense sadness overtook us both. I felt as though my little world was crashing down around me. I was once again alone. Why did the ones I love always leave me behind? My dad had left me, figuratively for my brother, Jay Jay and Macho had left me, and now my best friend was leaving. I felt so forlorn. I remember telling her goodbye through tears and hugs. Her mother finally pried us apart and ordered Tracy into the car saying, "Years from now, you girls will look back on this and see how silly you were being." We never did. Tracy would truly be my very best friend forever and ever.

After Tracy left, I never really had another close girlfriend. I had many friends and one who called herself my best friend, but I didn't really like anyone else. Teen girls can be so mean and catty. I had learned from experience that you couldn't trust any of them, so I kept them out of my heart and was only friends with them on the surface. My emotions were raw, and everything seemed like too much to deal with. I was nervously starting high school, no longer had a true friend, and my parents were strict, unfair and unenlightened concerning the modern world. My despair dipped so low that after one infuriating altercation with them, I sat alone on the floor of my room and considered suicide. I felt so powerless and utterly at their will. I had no say in my life and the decisions that they were making for me. I disagreed with their decisions but it didn't matter, I had no voice and they were unreasonable. When asked to explain their reasons why things had to be as they said, their answer was simply, "Because I said so." This angered me beyond belief. I had a mind of my own with thoughts of my own and felt I should have a say in my own life. I rationalized in my immature fourteen-year-old mind that I would show them. They would be sorry after I was dead. Luckily, the reasoning centers of my brain were developed enough to think this decision through and to realize that killing myself would indeed make them pay. They would be sorry, but then this crazy, sometimes difficult, life would also be over for me. I would never be able to do what I wanted to do because I would no longer be. I wisely decided to learn to deal with my frustrations and not check out.

I went back to the obedient quiet child who did as she was told to maintain peace in my home. I solitarily went through that freshman year of high school, keeping a safe distance from the mean girls and being only a superficial friend. There was one boy I considered a friend and I determined again that I should have been born a boy. Their lives seemed to be so much easier and were devoid of all the drama that teenage girls must endure. Boys seemed much more trustworthy than girls and they were beginning to pay more and more attention to me. There was one boy who was giving me a little too much attention for my liking, bordering on harassment. Every day, he would pinch me, trip me or punch me on the arm. I tried to avoid him, but he seemed to always find me. I rarely got new clothes, but one day I was wearing the uncommon new shirt. I was so proud of it because it had taken weeks of negotiation to convince my mother that I needed it. It was a yellow button-down oxford shirt with a fashionable loop on the back. I was feeling very pretty in my contemporary tunic, but those feelings would soon turn to anguish as my tormentor came up behind me, hooked his finger through the loop and gave it a sharp yank ripping the loop halfway off of the shirt. This was the final straw. Something had to be done to put an end to my persecution. I told my mom when I got home from school that day and her answer was quite perplexing. She told me that she did not think he was intentionally being mean to me, rather she suspected that he liked me. What a moronic way to demonstrate adoration! I was thoroughly puzzled. It seemed senseless to me that anyone would be mean to someone they liked. Toward the end of my freshman year, I was called to the office and informed that I was tied for Valedictorian honors. I didn't know what this meant but I immediately wanted to win this title. Maybe if I were the top in my class my parents would then be proud of me. I determined at that time I would get only A's in high school.

The strife at home continued as I struggled to have thoughts and ideas of my own. My loving parents seemed very controlling and having any conviction that differed from theirs was not received well. They didn't like the music I listened to, the friends I brought around, the things I liked. I interpreted this to mean, they didn't like me. I often felt as though I must have been adopted because I certainly did not fit in here. After one exasperating argument, I needed to get away for a while, so I took off indignantly walking down the railroad tracks. I had nowhere to go, but at that point, anywhere I ended up would be better than being in the presence of those intolerable closed-minded people who professed to have given me life. I angrily marched on, mumbling to myself and paying no mind to the distance I had traveled. As I contemplated my unbearable existence, I abruptly was dive bombed by a troop of skilled fighter pilots, aka red winged blackbirds, whose primary mission was to engage in air-to-ground combat with the intruder who threatened their homeland, namely me. I ducked and dodged their attack as I frantically attempted to evade their assault. I am an animal lover at heart, but had I possessed a missile, I surely would have fired it at them in a counterattack. Unfortunately, I came totally unprepared for this, so my only option was to flee. Retreat would have been a better option but without thinking I ran forward, going further from my house. I had no concept of how far I had run when I finally came to my senses and realized I had lost them. As I struggled to catch my breath, I contemplated the situation I now found myself in. I was walking along a railroad track going away from my home. When I finished walking, I planned to turn around and follow the railroad track back to my home. I was now faced with a dilemma as the red winged kamikaze blackbirds were standing between my destination and me. I was too scared to go through another attack so deduced that if I kept walking away from my house, I would eventually come to a road that led out to the highway and could safely return home via the road and not have to face another attack. Little did I know that the birds were far less dangerous than the peril that was lurking down that road. Between the stress of my near-death experience and the length of my cross-country trek, I was nearly done in by the time I reached the highway and turned to begin my long journey home. Funny how the place I felt so determined to flee from, now seemed to beckon me back. As my worn feet stepped onto the seemingly eternal highway that loomed menacingly before me, I was filled with dread. Why had I not retreated instead of running further from my home? Sometimes I could make such bad choices. I engaged in a self-debasement session as I walked along and chided myself for my poor decision-making abilities. I was surprised to hear the crackling of gravel close behind me as a car slowly approached. A man whom I approximated to be in his late thirties, rolled down the passenger side window of his gray Chevy Vega and greeted me with a friendly smile asking what I was doing out here all alone. He spoke as though he knew me but as I foolishly leaned in to get a closer look, I couldn't figure out how. He didn't really look familiar. Maybe he was one of my dad's friends. He offered me a ride and as I looked down the long road that stretched out ahead of me, this option won the decision. I hopped into the car and as he pulled away, I quickly glanced around the vehicle in an attempt to place this neighborly stranger. I noticed first a beer that he was slurping as though it were water in a desert. My eyes then scanned the back seat where the floorboard was littered with at least ten more empty ones. I ascertained that my dad most certainly did not know this man. He would not associate with one who drank beer. I had been schooled on the evils of alcohol and the things it made you do, terrible things that you normally would not do. My heart began to race as I realized what I had done. I had imprudently gotten into the car of a perfect stranger who obviously had been drinking for quite some time and now I was at his mercy. I concluded that he would take me away, rape me and kill me. I would never see my parents again. I began fervently whispering a silent prayer for God to deliver me from this deviant's hand. As we neared the road to my house, I nervously announced that he should begin slowing down because we were getting close to home. I made the decision that I would not take him to my house. If he wanted to kill someone, it should only be me. My family did not deserve to have this depraved man ascend onto their home. I doubtfully directed him to pull over in front of the abandoned filling station that sat at the end of my street and to my great surprise he began slowing the car. Before he even came to a complete stop, I threw open the door and sprang from the car yelling thanks and bolted the two blocks to my home, never daring to look back. As the adrenaline pulsed through my body, I sprinted up to my room and collapsed into the safety of my soft bed. My flowery lavender bed spread never looked so good. I thanked God for saving me and for getting me out of the perilous situation I had gotten myself into. I never spoke of this to my parents. I was too ashamed of my lack of wisdom on this day but for the first time in my life, I realized without a doubt, that even as I was making bad choices, God had been looking out for me and taking care of me.

As I approached dating age my suitors grew exponentially. There were many boys attempting to court me and one attractive older boy from a neighboring school caught my fancy. He was content to wait out my maturation to my liberating sixteenth birthday when I would at last be able to date. It was fun to have the attention of an older boy and I was thrilled when on the day of my first date ever, he brought me a dozen red roses. He seemed to know the way to my heart, but he also knew the way into a whole new world for me. My life thus far had been sheltered. There were never any drugs or alcohol in my home or in the home of my friends, but I was exposed to these elements extremely quickly with my newfound freedom. I remember walking through a party with Adam and seeing kids my age drinking a beer. I had been warned of the dangers of beer and wanted nothing to do with losing control of my mind and doing things I normally wouldn't do. I also noticed some kids sitting around in a circle on the floor. They had a glass pipe and were smoking something out of it. Although I had never been instructed on the dangers of drugs, instinct told me that this too was bad. I nervously waited for this night to be over. This was not a world I was familiar with nor did I want to be. Our courtship was short lived, and had it not been so close to the prom, it probably would have even been shorter. He kept me around until after the big night and then dumped me flat, sending a message through a common friend that he was afraid of hurting me because he had found himself wanting to do things that I was just not ready for. The message came through loud and clear. I was dumped because I wasn't ready for sex. I somehow felt that he had done the honorable thing by me and he was right. If that was what he wanted he needed to look elsewhere. It wasn't happening here. The only person I was having sex with was my husband.

I dated a few guys a couple of times, but no one really held my attention until a really cute boy from my art class, Brandon, started talking to me a lot. He was my type. Dark hair, dark eyes and muscles to die for. He was a charmer, always doing things to make me feel special. He would leave notes in my art box for me to find the next day saying things like, "You are one in a million." I was infatuated with this boy and when he got his driver's license, I was the first one he called to ask on a date. From that point on we were an item. Anything I wanted, he would give me. He went to church with me, even though he hadn't been raised in church. Anything I disliked, he disliked. I was amazed at how alike we were. He became very protective of me, reminiscent of Macho, my protector from earlier in life. No one would dare mess with me now. When we were out on a date, if another guy so much as looked my way he would menacingly bow up and start toward them and they would immediately cower and look away. I foolishly found this endearing. How flattering that he would be willing to fight for me. Unbeknownst to me, he did get in several altercations, to defend my honor, but I didn't hear of them until many years later. Had I only known of his true temperament, I may have made different choices, but around me he was always the perfect gentleman. I was clueless as to what he was capable of. I fell madly in love with him, or with the façade he presented me.

Brandon became my refuge from the storms that were brewing at home. My parents tried to warn me of the danger I was putting myself in. They warned me that I needed to choose wisely when deciding who I would spend the rest of my life with. I was incensed that they thought I was unable to choose wisely whom I wanted to marry. Their valid points were all discredited. I didn't care that he wasn't raised in a Christian home like I had been. They were nice to me and, besides, I wasn't planning to marry his family. I didn't care that he had juvenile diabetes. Did that mean, that he didn't deserve to have a wife and family someday? I was indignant at their cruelty, as my mother compared him to the runts of the litters that were always my favorite when choosing a pet. This was not the same thing. Yes, I did gravitate toward the weak little runts, whom I could love and save giving them a chance in life, but he was not a kitten or a puppy, he was a person who deserved to be loved and they were being insensitive and judgmental. I also was indignant that they didn't want me to be with him because he was not a Christian. Who were they to judge? The Bible says, "Judge not lest you be judged." He was right beside me every Sunday in church. God could save him. Maybe God was going to use me to be that influence in his life and help him come to God. I had no doubt that I could change that one. Eventually he would come around, of that I was certain.

I disappointedly wondered why it didn't seem to matter what I did; it was never good enough for my parents. I felt as though I was never the child my parents wanted me to be and their efforts to turn me into that child were met with fierce resistance as I grew older and more confident. My plans were to go off to California and attend art school after high school. I had dreams of becoming a graphic artist. Once again, as many times before in my life, my ideas were met with that "no" that was not to be argued with. Their plans were for me to go to Taylor University, a Christian college, and that was not up for discussion. I now realize how scary it must have been to think of their child moving that far away when they had never moved more than 20 minutes from their childhood homes, but at the time I was excited to get out and explore the world. I begrudgingly researched their school of choice and found no majors that interested me. I finally settled on becoming a kindergarten teacher. I did love children. These were a little older than my favorite two-year-old child, but out of all of my options at Taylor this seemed like the best. After years of hard work, I was poised to graduate at the top of my class and found that many scholarships came along with this honor. I had done all the right things, was a member of Honor Society, had taken the SAT and had been readily accepted into the university of my parent's choice. It appeared I had the world by the tail but inside I was not happy. I was living their dream. I felt that the only way they would love me was if I did as I was told and I so wanted them to love me.

I eventually resolved myself to my parent's choice for my future but for some reason Brandon wasn't very excited for me. He didn't really want to talk about college. He had no interest in furthering his education and was not very interested in me furthering mine. After about six months of dating exclusively, he finally said those words. He loved me. What a feeling! He loved me. The only people who had ever told me that were my family and now it seemed they were never happy with me. Brandon thought I was wonderful. He always accepted me and wanted me. I loved that he loved me and thought I could do no wrong. For some time now he had been pressuring me to take things further. He wanted sex but this conflicted with my basic moral system. I believed in my heart that I was not supposed to have sex until I was married but I did want him to be happy. My mind drifted back to that first boyfriend who moved on because I wasn't ready. Would Brandon move on too? I lost everyone who mattered to me in my life. First my dad abandoned me for my brother, then Jay Jay died, Macho was put to sleep and then Tracy moved away. Was Brandon the next to walk away? I tried my best to find a way to make this work so everyone would be happy. He did tell me he loved me, and it looked like we would one day be married. Technically, I would only be having sex with my husband because I intended to marry him. By twisting my thoughts around I eventually concluded that sex, in this case, would be ok.

In the broad scheme of things, what did it really matter if we did it now, or in a few years? I now know that having sex results in the release of a hormone called oxytocin. This hormone does several things that matter when it comes to a young girl's ability to logically reason. It lowers her defenses and increases trust while at the same time increases empathy. In other words, this hormone decreases a young girl's ability to clearly see a situation for what it is. It blurs the lines, so to speak. For a young Christian girl who has been taught that you only have sex with your husband, having sex also seals the deal for marriage in her mind. It takes away her options. I had made a decision, at 17 years of age, that I was not ready to make, no matter how grown I thought I was.

In approximately six months I turned up pregnant. I didn't understand how this could be. We always used protection. What I didn't know was that out of uneasiness about my pending departure for Taylor University, Brandon had devised a way to keep me home. Years later in a failed attempt to demonstrate how much "smarter" he was than I, he bragged of how he had discretely sabotaged a condom and I hadn't had a clue. So now here we were. He was perceptive. I will give him that. I longed to get away from my miserable teenage life, which included him, and go off to college to see what else there was in this world. There surely had to be more than I was seeing in Losantville, Indiana. I knew I had given away my right to meet a fine young Christian man in college and live happily ever after, but I secretly hoped that maybe God would forgive me if I didn't marry the boy I had slept with. I wanted to get away from this small town where everyone was all in your business and where I had to be perfect so as not to embarrass my family. The pressures of being perfect and keeping everyone happy were wearing on me, and I was looking forward to making my escape. There now would be no escape. I was pregnant and every morning I would wake wishing it were all just a nightmare, but it wasn't. It was real.

It was the spring of my senior year and what looked to those around me like a charmed perfect life, was threatening to crumble to the ground. I was too scared to tell my parents and so I went along for three months, pretending that the little life growing inside of me didn't exist. My mother was much too astute to let this one slip by her and she went into private investigator mode, scouring over my room when I was away at school during the day. I guess if you look hard enough, you are likely going to find what you are looking for and she did. She found a note with sexual connotations in it between Brandon and me. On that fateful Friday evening I was preparing for our usual date night when my parents asked to see me in the living room. As I cluelessly sauntered into the room, it was immediately evident that something was wrong. I don't remember too much about that conversation other than the anger I saw in my daddy's eyes as he inquired about my lovers. He stormed from the room going to get his gun to kill the boy who had violated his little girl. I screamed in fear. Would my father kill the father of my child? In the ensuing chaos, my mother asked me if I was pregnant. She quickly left me standing dazed in the living room and went to stop my dad. As she told him the news he began to wail. It was a sound I had never heard before and hope to never hear again. It was the sound of a father mourning the loss of the innocence of his perfect little girl. I covered my ears but could not drown out the horrific sound of my dad's heartbreaking sorrow.

My senior picture. Looks like I am ready to take on the world. I had no clue what was coming.

4
LIFE-ALTERING MISTAKE

My life would be forever changed because of the poor decision of a naïve rebellious 17-year-old girl longing for acceptance. Don't get me wrong, I blame only myself for the decisions I made. I only say that to explain that I now have great clarity as to how those choices became options in my less than fully developed mind. You see I had let myself get too close to danger. Even though I knew right from wrong, I foolishly thought I could play close to the fire and not get burned. Little did I know that if you hang around with anyone for too long you develop feelings for that person whether you intend to or not, and then those feelings cloud your judgment and I wound up doing things I never planned to do with someone I was never meant to do them with. I planned to go off to college, get my degree, meet the man I was supposed to marry and live happily ever after. Instead, I was now stuck in Hicksville, a baby having a baby, with a young boy who shared none of my basic moral values, embarking on the darkest season of my life. I wonder if God was as heartbroken as my earthly daddy? The sound of his crying was the most horrific sound I had ever heard and, try as I might, I could not unhear it.

While my dad was heartsick, my mother was angry. How dare I embarrass her in this way? She had raised me better than this and now she was humiliated. How would she face her friends? It seemed she had determined that the best course of action was to punish me for my insurrection by making my life miserable. I was waking up in my same bed, sitting at the same table and living in the same house but my mother would neither look at me, nor talk to me. I lived for weeks in silent torture, dealing with the now full on rejection of my mother. Even though, one of the adults in my life had discreetly suggested an abortion, that was not a viable option in my mind. I finally determined that when I turned 18, in another month I would just be married and get out of this place. This home that had once been my safe harbor was now filled with misery and disappointment. I felt I had let my parents down and as long as I was living in their home, there was no escaping the finality and reality of that.

I went about planning my escape. It was February of 1984. That year I was to graduate with honors, Valedictorian of my senior class but all I wanted to do was disappear. The social stigma was enough to make me want to run away and never face my friends again. I told no one, but in a small-town, secrets don't keep long. We went to a remote hospital in a neighboring town to do the blood tests for our marriage license in the hopes that the event would remain covert. But as fate would have it, we ran into someone we knew, Pam. Of all people, why did it have to be her? My heart sank as I realized that my undisclosed indiscretion would soon be public knowledge. The next day at school, it was apparent that my private nightmare had become public knowledge. As I walked solitarily down that long, lonely high school hallway, I could hear the vicious whispers and see the judgmental heads turn as I passed. This only served to further isolate me and further drove my desire to escape my intolerable situation. Why do people seem to enjoy the misfortune of others? There were no sympathetic peers or adults coming to me with care or concern. The only thing I got was further denunciation and degradation. I was called into the principal's office later that day and asked to resign the position I had earned in the National Honor Society. I had worked so hard to receive only A's throughout my entire educational career and felt that I had earned that honor. The principal explained to me that what I had done was not very honorable and that I did not deserve to be associated with students who were doing the right thing. How could I argue with that? My spirit was crushed. Toward the end of the day I was called into the guidance office. One would think that a person in this position of guiding young adults as they planned their way in the world would have had some edifying advice, but this was not so. She advised me to give up all the scholarships that I had been awarded to further my education and ensure my future. She reasoned that now that I was pregnant, I had no future. I was destined to never amount to anything more than an indigent burden on society; therefore, those dollars should go to someone who at least had a hope of a future. By this time, I had no more fight left in me. I conceded and left her office more beat down and dejected than I had ever been in my entire 17 years of life. I had no one to blame but myself. I was so stupid to have made this choice and to have let this happen. Now my life was essentially over. I had broken my daddy's heart, my mother wasn't speaking to me, my mentors at school were disavowing me and my peers had seemingly already castigated me. So quickly that privileged girl with everything was reduced to nothing. I went into survival mode. If I could just get through these last three months of school, get married and move away from home, I would be free from all of the condemnation. As I drudged through the days, a small ray of hope came from my father. For years I had always gotten ready for school and on my way out the door would stop by my dad's bedroom, to wake him and tell him good-bye but my typical morning routine had been discontinued, due to the fact that I thought my dad wanted nothing to do with this disgraceful child he had raised. On one life altering morning as I quietly tiptoed by him to leave, he stopped me and called me to him. I took a deep breath as I approached, dreading the chiding that was to come. He handed me an envelope with $1,800 in it, my parent's tax return for that year. He explained that having a baby was expensive and that he wanted me to use the money to get a good doctor. The money was not the life changing part of this exchange, but rather what happened next. As I sat beside him on the bed trying to understand this kind gesture, I looked up to see tears forming in his soft blue eyes. I prayed he wouldn't start crying again. My heart couldn't take it. But the tears this time were tears of pure love as he reached up, took me into those strong loving arms once again and whispered, "No matter what, I love you and you will always be my baby." Oh, how I needed that love and acceptance at that moment. Even if I had made a mess of my life, my daddy still loved me.

As was the custom with girls who found themselves in my predicament, we were quickly married. As I had planned, we waited until I had turned 18 to avoid the awkwardness of asking my parents for permission. I am sure they would have given it. After all, they were anxious to make this right and if you were to have a baby, you must be married. With both of us still in high school neither had a job so we moved in with his parents and lived in the basement of their house. I quickly found out that until you live with someone, you don't really know them. I knew that his family was different from mine, but they had always seemed very accepting of me, until I moved into their basement. Once I was living under their roof, they no longer seemed to like me. I was yelled at and cussed out for not living up to their expectations of me. Sometimes his mom would get a scary look in her eyes that I had never seen before. I wondered what was worse, living in silence in my own home or this. I reasoned that in a couple of months we would graduate, and Brandon could start work. At that point we could get our own house and I would no longer be subjected to this. I began to sense that this family was a bit volatile and I wondered what all he had been through as a child. He kept his family secrets very well and seldom discussed them. On one occasion, he let his guard down and told me about incidents of rage, violence, and things being broken in the house and that he, as a small boy, went about trying to restore everything. This was shocking to me because my home had always been a place of safety. When I pressed Brandon for more information, he shut down. He began denying everything he had told me and said he should have never brought it up. He would never speak of those family secrets again.

They say the apple doesn't fall far from the tree and it wasn't long before I got to see this firsthand. It was a sunny Saturday afternoon and we were sitting out on the back deck enjoying the warm breeze and watching my collie, Sabin, run and play. He truly was majestic. He was the grandest collie I had ever known and even though he didn't have what it took to be a show dog, he worked out just fine as my buddy. After throwing the ball and enjoying a lively game of chase, Sabin ran up to the deck, putting his front legs on mine and began showering me with slobbery kisses to thank me for loving him and playing with him. I loved him so much and was in heaven hugging and petting him. I marveled that there is nothing quite as pure as a dog's love for his master and I only wished I could be as good of a person as he thought I was. He was so loving, gentle and loyal and as his long fur surrounded my face I was snapped back to reality as Brandon's fist came flying in between us and landed squarely into Sabin's unsuspecting head. As Sabin staggered and struggled to stand on his feet I shrieked with disbelief, "Why would you do that?" Brandon's reply puzzled me. He said it was because I acted like I wanted to have sex with the dog. I was bewildered and absolutely confused. I never knew people might punch an innocent dog in the head. I had heard stories about that crazy guy in school who tortured cats, but I thought they were just stories, kids making stuff up to have something to talk about. I never knew someone could be cruel to an animal. I did know that I would not subject Sabin to this and if Brandon were going to act this way then Sabin would go back to my parent's house. I promptly took him back home and explained to my mom that we couldn't take care of him. I cautiously broached the subject about Brandon being mean to get some perspective on this and was promptly shut down. My mother abruptly told me not to tell her about the problems in my marriage because I would forgive him and go back to him, but she wouldn't be able to. It would be another 13 years before I would attempt to ask her for help again. She had made her position known.

And so began my life of trying to make Brandon happy. He had acted out of jealousy. I was giving the dog more attention than I was giving him, so I must do better. If I only showed him well enough how much I love him, I reasoned, he would not have the need to have these senseless outbursts. I would fix him. I would save him from the pain his family had imposed upon him. There was no other option. When you married, it was for life and the only thing more shameful than being pregnant out of wedlock would be to fail at holding together God's most sacred union. I had said the vows, for better or worse, right there in the church in front of God and my family. I was in this til death do us part. I sucked it up, finished school and graduated at the top of my class. The honor cords had been ordered months before I had "dishonored" myself and my peers, so I defiantly wore them on graduation night. It was not announced that I had been inducted into the National Honor Society but the cords around my neck said that I had. As I walked up to the podium, I thought about how those stupid cords really didn't matter. The fact that as the valedictorian, I was giving a speech really didn't matter. Everyone knew what I had done and that I had ruined my life with my adolescent failings. I was ashamed as I stepped up and began speaking. Nothing I said mattered. Why would anyone listen to someone as shameless and brainless as me?

It felt good to close the book on that part of my life. I wanted it to be over. I could now start my adult life as a wife and mother. Surely, I wouldn't screw that up. Brandon secured a job at a local machine shop and we were able to move into our first home. We had saved up the first month's rent of $125 and the required $100 deposit and were anxious to set up house. The home was a two-story white-washed home built somewhere around 1900. It had the original hardwood floors, mold behind the fresh white paint on the walls, and large windows that allowed the cold winter wind to creep in, but it was home. Luckily the house was right next door to my sister and her husband, and she too was expecting. For the first time in our lives we had something in common. She had done things the right way, as always. She married a man with good Christian morals who was a member of our church and then made a conscious decision to have a child. I wished I wasn't such a screw up and could have been more perfect like her. I could never tell her about my husband's shortcomings. She couldn't possibly understand when her life was so perfect. So, I put on my best smile and did as I had been taught all my life. I didn't air my dirty laundry. No one knew what was going on behind closed doors. This charming young man who swept me off my feet at 16 years of age was no longer the sweet and loving guy from high school who would do anything for me and thought I did no wrong. Quite the opposite, I seemingly could do nothing right. He was never happy with me. He began quizzing me accusingly about my checkups at the OBGYN. He always wanted to know if the doctor had touched me and after being accused of enjoying it, I started lying and told him that the doctor was only listening to the baby's heartbeat through my belly. I didn't like lying to my husband, but it seemed when I told the truth about it a crazy switch would be flipped inside of his head and he would go out of his mind with jealousy. It appeared that my mother was right when she had warned of her pity for the man I would eventually marry. It seemed, I was a terrible wife. My husband was always angry. He demanded that his castle be kept spotless. I tried to be perfect, but nothing satisfied him. I had been taught that the Bible says to not let the sun go down upon your wrath, but he didn't believe in the Bible and when I tried to talk things out before going to bed, that only served to infuriate him. Many nights I spent scrubbing the floors, doing dishes and dusting through my tears into the wee hours of the morning, to try to bring him happiness, all to no avail. His anger came from somewhere deep inside of him that I could not reach, no matter how hard I tried, but oh how I tried. I cooked him three meals a day, cleaned continuously and doted on him every moment he was home. Most of the time this worked...until the baby arrived.

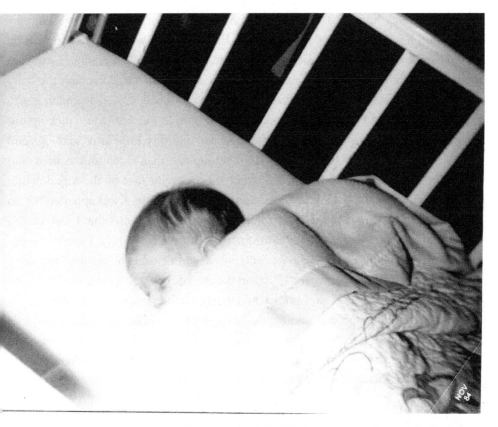

Monty one month old.

Monty came into this world on October 1, 1984 weighing 6 pounds and 2 ounces after 18 hours of hard labor. He had a whole head full of hair and was so tiny and precious as he looked around wide-eyed in the delivery room. I instantly fell in love with this little one who was totally dependent on me for everything. I knew beyond a shadow of a doubt that I had at least done one thing right in making the decision to keep this sweet baby boy and I vowed to raise him the right way and give him the kind of home that I had grown up in. I couldn't wait to rock him to sleep while singing to him, but Monty wasn't the rocking type. I remember trying ardently to rock my baby into peaceful slumber, but he would fuss, fidget and whimper until I laid him down in his bed where he would go instantly to sleep. To my dismay, it was apparent very early on that he was not the snuggling type. The time it requires to care for a newborn baby is not compatible with taking care of the needs of an angry, insecure man. Babies require much attention and that was attention that Brandon needed. He was immediately jealous of any time I spent with our newborn baby and would hound me mercilessly about it. Breastfeeding was nearly more that he could handle because, to him, it signified some sort of sexual perversion. I was torn between trying to give my husband the attention he needed and keeping the baby from crying. When Monty squeaked, I learned to jump because if Brandon got to him first, his way of handling it was quite disturbing to me. He would pick up our tiny fragile little one, with his wobbly little head and tiny little arms and legs and throw him nearly to the top of our 12-foot ceiling and then catch him as he would free fall back down. He had found that when the air hit his face on the way down, it would take his breath away and momentarily stop the crying. I was appalled but no amount of discussing it could change it. His response was always that I just wanted to raise a sissy boy and that no son of his was going to be a sissy. I secretly wondered if I was being overprotective, but I just couldn't bear the sight of my newborn, in all of his fragility, flying 12 feet in the air. I developed a system of trying to keep Monty from crying, but if I failed and the inevitable happened, I would simply step in, demand he stop and remove the baby from him. The astonishment of this unexpected way of handling a newborn baby soon became the norm and ceased to shock me. When prevention didn't work, I became like the FEMA workers who go in after the fact and fix whatever had gone wrong. This became the fabric of my life.

In high school it seemed we were perfect for each other. How could I have been so mistaken? We now had nothing in common. I wanted to protect and nurture our newborn baby. He wanted to make a man of him. I wanted to talk out our differences and make things okay again. He wanted to roll over, go to sleep and forget they existed. I wanted to abstain from taking in any substance that would harm my body or impair my brain function. I had been taught to fear alcohol. He thought drinking was a great stress reliever. I wanted to pay all our bills before they came due. He wanted to live in the here-and-now and worry about the light bill if they came to turn it off. I wanted God at the center of my life. He had no use for God. I tried so hard to minimize the conflict and to keep him happy, but little did I know that was an unobtainable goal. While I seemed to have no influence on what he did or didn't do, I was determined to not let him keep me from what I knew to be right. I continued to cling to the teaching of my youth and go to church every time the doors were open while he either slept in or headed to the garage to drink with his buddies. One Wednesday evening, when Monty and I were gone to church, an old girlfriend of mine from high school stopped by to see me. Brandon invited her in to visit anyway and when I arrived home, I could feel the tension in the air. This was a new feeling for me and I struggled to make sense of it. He finally excused himself and she whispered to me that he had tried to kiss her. This notion struck me as quite bizarre. Why would she make something like that up? He was my husband and I firmly believed I was now the only one he wanted to kiss. Her claim was simply an act of pure jealousy. She was not married with a family and she must be jealous. Why else would she say something so preposterous? When I told him of her lies, he reassured me that I had nothing to worry about and I foolishly believed him wholeheartedly. To prove his love for me, the next day he arrived home from work with two tiny baby kittens. They were gray tiger striped and were little balls of fuzz. They couldn't have been more than 5 weeks old and they did the trick. They instantly melted my heart. As always, these sweet precious animals snuggled in close to me and gave me that unconditional love I so needed.

The breakdown of the mother and daughter relationship and the ensuing silent treatment was never addressed, but my mother eventually began coming around. As I worked diligently to fulfill my new role of wife and mother, she would come to pick me up once a week and we would go to the grocery together. One sunny afternoon as we returned home, we noticed flashing lights ahead and cars lined up with no one being allowed to pass. Simultaneously we noticed that the flashing lights appeared to be at my grandparent's house. We jumped out of the car and began hurriedly making our way past the stopped cars and emergency vehicles to the house to see what was going on. My grandfather, who we called Papaw, had been out burning the fencerow. The fire had begun to get a bit out of control, and he thought it best to climb over the fence to stamp it out with his boots. As he attempted to do this, a firefighter was driving by, and stopped to see if he could be of assistance. Papaw's boot became stuck on the fence and before the fireman could get to him, he was engulfed in flames. The fireman watched as the horrendous fire consumed him as he stood on the fence. Then as quickly as it started, the fireman reported seeing a white form ascend from his body into the heavens and my grandfather's earthly body fell to the ground. At 84 years of age my grandfather was gone. We were told that no one had gone into the house to let my grandmother know so we made our way in. She was in the early stages of Alzheimer's and had not even noticed the commotion outside. We somberly told her what had happened. For the first of probably hundreds of times, the family tried to explain to her that "daddy" as she called him, would not be coming home. Each time she was told it was as if she were hearing it for the first time. How was she going to survive now without him to care for her? As it turned out, the children they had raised so well together, stepped up in a big way and each of the seven took one day a week to stay with her in her own home, to see that she was taken care of. They would continue this act of utter love and selflessness until it was no longer possible to provide the care she needed, then they would be forced to turn over her care to a skilled nursing facility. Life around me was crumbling. My grandparents were no longer the visible strong and stable cornerstone of my family, but their strong Christian legacy could never be destroyed.

Back at home, church quickly became a battleground for us. I was holding firmly to the religious expectations but Brandon did not share my beliefs. Not only did he refuse to go to church but he decided I didn't need to go either. He wanted me to stay home with him. I am ashamed to admit that my going to church had nothing to do with my love of God. Rather, I was going because that is what I was supposed to do. At this point in my life I didn't really get God. I knew right from wrong and I was a rule follower. I had been taught that when the church doors were open, you went to church so that's what I was determined to do. One night when I was at church with Monty, Brandon became enraged that I had taken our son and was sitting in church with my parents and my friends rather than at home waiting on him. When I returned home, he arrogantly told me about what I had caused him to do. He reasoned that I would rather spend time with them than with him, and he wanted to pay me back. He wanted me to hurt as bad as I had hurt him. He boasted that as he paced angrily in the back yard trying to decide what to do, he heard the faint meows of the defenseless baby kittens he had brought home to me a few days before and decided they would suffice. That would surely make me think twice before leaving him alone again. In a rage he had picked the kittens up and flung them with all his might against the outside garage wall, instantly crushing their skulls and ending their lives. I was horrified and this revelation was so heinous in my mind that I never thought of it again for 12 years. For me it was as though it never happened. This unspeakable act disappeared from my memory and went to dwell with the first act of animal cruelty, somewhere deep in my subconscious. I am sure the memory was always in there, controlling my actions to some extent, but some way, somehow it disappeared from the surface.

In hindsight, maybe me going to church and leaving him was one of his triggers. Bad things always seemed to happen when I went to church. The first time I discovered his drinking came on the cusp of a church service. I had returned home to the sound of loud music and laughter coming from the garage. When I went to investigate, I found a handful of men surrounded by a sea of beer cans and bottles of whisky. I temporarily lost my mind. I threw the visitors out and proceeded to bust the glass bottles to pieces against the block walls insisting that no husband of mine would partake of this evil substance. Through tears I ranted and raved and demanded that this never happen again. To my knowledge it didn't. He became more discrete with his drinking and I never saw the evidence of it again.

He soon strategically moved our little family a little further out of town. Our new home was far enough away that I could no longer walk to church, to my sisters or to my mom's. This way, he would have much more control over me, and I would not go thinking I was in charge. The house was a little nicer but that meant it cost a little more. At this house I was extremely isolated. We only had one car, which he drove to work, and we had no phone half of the time due to not paying our bill, so I was stuck out in the middle of nowhere with no human contact, other than my baby. We were profoundly poor. Brandon was bringing home $150 a week and our ends were failing to meet. I oversaw paying all of the bills and the stress of it was overwhelming. There simply was never enough to pay them all. On the rare occasion when I dared confront him with a disconnect notice or overdue notice, he would become enraged, breaking things in the house, punching walls and screaming at me. I was to blame. What was I doing with all the money he gave me? Out of exasperation, I gave over the duty of paying the bills to him. At least now he would not have any reason to accuse me of wasting our money frivolously. He would see how there was not enough to go around. Things only got worse from there. He didn't worry about where the money was going to come from, he simply didn't pay. When the phone was disconnected, I was secretly kind of glad because I wouldn't have to deal with the constant hounding of the bill collectors anymore. The electricity being turned off was not so handy though, especially with a baby in the house and when his parents would get wind of it, they would pay to have it turned back on again. At this time in my life, the only access I had to money was the $20 a week that Brandon gave me for groceries. Diapers cost me $7 per week and that left $13 for food. I enjoyed going to the grocery because it was the one time I had a little freedom and could set foot out of the house. I would load up my baby and off we would go.

Brandon always insisted I take the baby with me which was just as well because I didn't trust him to be alone with our child. Our shopping trips were fun as Monty attempted to talk to and hug everyone we encountered. He was such a social little guy. This trait confounded me because I would have preferred to not have to speak to anyone ever. I was painfully shy and didn't want anyone to even look my way. This was exacerbated by the fact that I was always being accused of indiscretions, so it was just better to go unnoticed. Shopping with my remaining $13 dollars became a game of sorts. I became very adept at finding cheap meals and felt as though I had won when I had found 7 days' worth of meals for that price. I determined that we could have one meal per day and the main course could only cost $1. If you shop generic you could get hotdogs, grilled cheese, potato soup, bologna and peanut butter. There were lots of options for a dollar.

As time went by, Brandon's jealousy and insecurity rose to a whole new level. He refused to let me go anywhere alone. If he couldn't go, I, at the very least, had to take the baby. One day, we were all out and needed to stop for gas. As I attempted to exit the car to go in and use the restroom Brandon stopped me. He said I didn't need to go in the gas station, and I should just stay put in the car. When I inquired as to why, he explained that there were too many men inside and they might think I liked them. I searched his face to see if this were some kind of joke, but the look in his eyes told me immediately that it wasn't. He truly believed that those men were a threat to our marriage. I was baffled by his insecurities. I had never thought of cheating on him and never would. When I got married it was forever, for better or for worse and I was not about to break my vows. I learned to never look at people. It was best to just stare at the ground. That way he could never misconstrue my intentions and it end up in a blow up. I made the mistake of talking to an old classmate that we ran into once and that night I paid dearly for that mistake. The entire night was a tirade of misguided distrust. He paced the house, yelling at me with his fists clinched and the evilest look in his eyes I had ever seen. He told me that I had been flirting with this guy and asked me if I wanted to have sex with him. I was so confused. I couldn't understand where this came from. As I denied his accusations, he fumed that even if I didn't want to, that because of the way I was acting, this guy thought that I wanted to. He was humiliated that this old classmate of ours thinks if he wanted to take me to bed, he could. Everything I said to defend myself only served to enrage him further. As he mocked my words, he picked up a glass from the table and flung it across the room hitting the antique porcelain sculpture that was sitting on a shelf, shattering it into a million pieces. It was the one keepsake I had gotten from my grandma's estate after she had been placed in a nursing home and now it lay in pieces on the ground, irreparable. I slumped to the ground in tears trying to piece it back together but to no avail. His wrath eventually ran out of steam and he settled down for the night and all was well again. I never understood how he could be so violent and mean and then act as though nothing had happened. The next day he would go about his business as usual, as though he had not been an out of control mad man the night before. I left the shattered glass laying there on the ground for weeks, refusing to clean up the ridiculous mess that stemmed from his irrational insecurities, thinking that he may gain some insight into how violent and scary his behavior was, but he never acknowledged the event and I eventually gave in and cleaned it up.

Most of the time, we would have about a two-week honeymoon period in between blowups where everything would be peaceful, and I would begin believing that I had finally figured out how to make him happy. Everything I did was with him in mind. When I chose what food to cook, cleaned the house, chose my clothes, it was all an attempt to keep him happy. So, the day that I laid out in the back yard on an old rusted lawn chair to get a suntan was an effort to look better for him, but somehow, I messed that up as well. He returned home from work that day in a rage. He claimed that someone had shown up at work that day with pictures of me laying out topless, and now all his coworkers had seen me naked and thought I was a slut. That assertion was ludicrous. I wouldn't dream of laying out topless, but as usual there was no convincing him. The evening was full of yelling, calling me degrading names and punching walls to intimidate me into acting the way he wanted. I was so confused. I didn't understand how I could be such a failure at this marriage thing. I had always been pretty good at whatever I set my mind to doing but I couldn't seem to conquer this one. I would have to try harder and be more careful. Because of my supposed indiscretion that day, Brandon devised a plan to keep better control of me.

That plan was Penny, the guard dog. She was a full-grown, pit bull that hated women. I attempted to make friends with her, but her low growl and bared teeth warned me that it would be ill advised. Her home became the wrap around porch that surrounded our house and she became the guard that kept me in. I could no longer set foot safely outside of my house. I was a prisoner in my own home. I was dealing with the fact that I could no longer leave the house because I had no car.

I was even accepting that I couldn't talk to my friends or family because we had no phone. But not being able to walk outside in the grass and feel the sunshine on my skin was torturous for me. I loved being outside but would have to learn to live without it. Sometimes in life, what the devil means for bad, God turns around and uses for good and late one night that is exactly what happened. I was home alone and noticed a car had pulled up in front of my house. Eventually two men knocked on the door and asked to come in to use my phone. They explained that their radiator had a leak and needed to call for help. Penny, the guard dog stood nervously on the porch forming a barrier between the men and myself. They asked to use my phone and I explained that I didn't have one. They nervously eyed the growling pit bull with the hair standing up on the back of her neck and asked if she would bite. I told them she would but that I might be able to pass some water for their radiator over to them. They shuffled their feet and stammered around looking apprehensively at each other and at the unrestrained dog that stood between them and what they wanted. They finally conceded to the water and I went to fill an empty milk jug with water from the faucet. When I returned, the men were gone. Apparently, their car began working again and they were able to move on down the road to find another victim who didn't have a guardian angel in the form of a pit bull watching over them.

We were living a life of little to no luxury often not even having the essentials. Luckily, the government has a system in place to return tax money to those living at or below the determined poverty level and at tax time, we got a decent refund. I was excited thinking about all the items we needed but had been unable to buy due to lack of funds. Maybe now I could get a blanket for our bed or shoes for the baby or maybe just pay the bills to make them current. My husband, however, had other plans. He looked at the tax check as a vacation from work fund and chose to stay at home in bed until the money ran out. I felt as though I was losing my mind. I would never understand the way this man's mind worked. He told me to call his work and tell them he was sick, but I refused. I didn't want to lie but I also didn't want to enable this behavior. Work began calling, neither of us would answer and surprise of all surprises, he got fired. I was stressed out to the max. The bill collectors were calling, and he was taking a vacation in bed. Eventually, the money ran out and he dragged himself up out of bed and found another job. Amazingly, he was now making more than he was before. Depending on how much overtime he worked he would bring home between $350 and $500 per week. We felt rich, but even the increase in cash flow didn't curtail Brandon's seething anger and his insecurities seemed to be mounting. Following every blow up, Brandon felt the need to reconnect by reclaiming his wife. I didn't dare let him know that I wasn't interested. If I refused him, he would really think I was getting my needs met elsewhere. I didn't understand how he thought I would want to be intimate after he had just yelled and screamed calling me every name in the book and accusing me of horrible things. Sex was the last thing I was interested in after a fight, but I guess it was never about what I wanted. It was about control. I would begrudgingly comply, and it is little wonder that when Monty was only six months old, I turned up pregnant again. I naively thought that since I was breastfeeding, I wouldn't get pregnant. I was mistaken. I went into a depression. I wasn't ready for another baby. I felt like a frazzled circus clown trying to juggle and was struggling trying to keep all the balls in the air. I had to keep a spotless house, keep the baby from crying, and keep my husband's jealousy at bay and now I was pregnant again. How could I possibly cope with two babies at one time and how would we pay for two children. There was no way the measly $20 a week that I got for groceries was going to cut it if I had to buy two boxes of diapers out of that.

Monty was a very precocious child and was always on the move. He learned to walk at seven months of age and was off to the races. It was apparent early on that he was going to be a strong-willed child. I remember a very early incident with the trashcan. He found it amusing to tip it over and dump the trash out on the floor. I did not think it was amusing and told him "no, no" in my sweet mommy voice. He laughed and did it again. I picked up the trash again and this time said with a little more authority, "No." He laughed and did it again. I tried removing him from the situation, but he quickly returned to the scene. He was determined to win this battle, as was I. Finally, out of desperation I swatted his little hand. He laughed again. He eventually got frustrated knowing he was about to get in trouble and would begin to cry as he reached for the trash to dump it. I sighed in exasperation. Raising this child was not going to be easy. Even though it was difficult to keep up with a seven-month-old baby who was walking while I was having all the side effects of pregnancy, I was learning that I was capable of much more than I ever imagined.

Being a first-time mom, I was hyper vigilant, reading everything I could get my hands on concerning raising a happy healthy child. I carefully followed all the latest information to be sure my baby was progressing as expected. He seemed to do everything early and this often got him into trouble. From day one, he was an early riser and when the sun was up, so was he. Our bedrooms were upstairs in the farmhouse we lived in and Monty's baby bed was against the wall adjoining ours. When he awoke in the wee hours of the morning, he would let us know by shaking the side railing of the baby bed, which made a very efficient alarm clock as it slammed into the wall and resonated into our room. Brandon had the bright idea to teach him to climb out of his bed when he woke up, obviously not thinking that one through. A ten-month-old baby has no business knowing how to remove himself from the safe confines of his baby bed. Once it was done, I had to deal with the consequences to avoid a fall down the 15 sharp and steep stairs that led down to the lower level. There was a railing, but being an old house, it wasn't built to standard and the rungs were just far enough apart for a 12-month-old baby to slip through. About the time he turned a year old, Monty decided to test the width of the rungs. As I walked out of my room that morning, all I could see was one little hand, holding on to one of the rungs. As I got closer, I could see that the rest of his body was dangling precariously over what would have been the longest drop to the bottom of the stairs. I couldn't reach through the railing to get ahold of him so I ran below him and instructed him to let go and Mommy would catch him. He trustingly did and giggled with delight as he fell safely into my arms. I hugged him tight and prayed a quick prayer of thanks to God for not allowing something terrible to happen. By the time Monty was 15 months old, and I was extremely pregnant, I read that a child of his age should be saying approximately 25 words. That seemed like a lot to me and I began a list of every word that he said unsolicited. After a few hours I gave up on the list and could rest assured that his vocabulary was in good shape because he had already come up with 128 words.

As concerned as I was with making sure my son had everything he needed for his future, my husband seemed equally unconcerned with securing our future. Even with his recent increase in pay we seemed to never have any money. With his newfound wealth, he felt the need to spend. We took out loan after loan buying a new mobile home to live in, a new car and a new truck for him. I worried about being over extended, but he didn't. Surely the bank looks at the income verses the outgoing and won't loan someone too much right? Wrong. He kept asking and they kept giving. We were soon strapped and stressed again. At least now I was not so isolated from the world. I had a car and I had a neighbor who was around my age. She had a daughter and was pregnant with her second. We quickly became friends as we had so much in common. With my neighbor as a distraction, I hardly even noticed when my husband started working later and later. I reasoned that it would mean a larger paycheck and, besides, things were more relaxed when he was away. Little did I know that this is when the affairs started. If I hadn't been so naïve, I might have figured it out. If I had paid attention to the difference between the hours he was away from home and the actual pay he was bringing home, I might have figured it out, but I didn't even think to mistrust him. If I wasn't so stupid, I might have picked up on the cashier at the grocery store who would ignore me and talk to Monty about how his daddy was doing and why he wasn't with us. I did find that strange and momentarily wondered why she would be asking a baby about his daddy. How would she even know his daddy? I shook the calamity off that was threatening to destroy my marriage and chose to not connect the dots. I couldn't get my mind to even go there. Marriage was forever. Infidelity was not an option and, besides, I had other things to think about. At just 20 years of age, I was about to become a mother of two.

5
FAILURE IS NOT AN OPTION

When the new baby came, my juggling act got even more difficult. Chad was born on Super Bowl Sunday in 1986. In an effort to avoid another 18 hours of labor in the hospital, I almost stayed home too long. We arrived at the hospital around 11:00 pm and I was doubtful when the nurse announced that I would have this baby before midnight. She was right, and after some quick work by the nurses, and a brief scare with the cord around his neck, he was born weighing 7 pounds and 2 ounces. From the onset it was apparent how different the two brothers, born from the same parents, could be. He frowned at the light, tried to keep his eyes closed whenever possible and immediately stuck his thumb in his mouth and went to sleep. He was a very good baby. Being a thumb sucker, he was very self-sufficient from the get-go. If he woke up, he simply stuck his thumb in his mouth and went back to sleep.

The joyful celebration of the arrival of my second child was short lived when my husband came into the hospital the second day with the announcement that he had quit his job. I was stunned. In what world is it an option to quit a job having no other source of income, one day after having a new baby? He was finally making decent money and the insurance was great. What if the kids needed medical attention? This seemed so foolish to me. Fear consumed me. How would we pay for two babies and all the loans we had taken out with no income? He wasn't concerned. He explained that it had to be done. His boss didn't understand how important it was to be with his family and wanted him to work rather than be at the hospital all day. According to my husband, his boss had the gall to tell him that he needed to get his priorities straight. Brandon reasoned that he did have his priorities straight and he showed him by quitting. Somehow, we made it through, as we always did, but little by little my husband was losing all respect from me. I thought the man of the house was someone who could be counted on to take care of things; that is who my father and my grandfather were. The man I had chosen, was not turning out to be such a person

When we brought the baby home, he was greeted very energetically from the former baby of the house, 15-month-old Monty who was now to take on the role of big brother. Monty had been anxiously awaiting his brother's arrival and wanted to play basketball with him. Immediately upon walking into the room, he threw a full-sized basketball into his bassinette. I took a deep breath as I diverted the ball from the tiny new baby and realized that taking care of two babies was going to be every bit as difficult as I had feared. Chad was much more laid back than Monty had been. Finally, I was able to rock my baby. Chad adored snuggling. He would sleep peacefully in my arms with his thumb and a blanket for hours. Well, I imagined that he would, but who had hours to rock a baby when there was a busy 15-month-old to chase after. The boys and I spent our days with the neighbor and her two girls, seeing less and less of their dad. Life was just easier when he was away. Brandon was always angry. I had learned to try to keep the children away from him, but sometimes that was hard. We were, after all, living in a small trailer. As I became an expert diverter, most of the bad experiences could be avoided, but every now and then something would happen that I didn't see coming. As was the case the day Monty was running through the living room and ventured too close to where his dad was apathetically parked on the couch watching television. For no better reason than pure nastiness, Brandon stuck out his foot and tripped him. He fell into the side of the couch and got a black eye. This was the first visible indicator of the abusive world we were living in. It was easy enough to explain away when people inquired about it. Monty was an extremely rambunctious child and so it wasn't much of a stretch to say he had fallen into the couch. He had fallen into the couch.

I just surreptitiously left out the part about him being helped by his father's foot. The ill will that this father had for his own family was unfathomable to me. Not that there is ever any justification for tripping a two-year-old, but Monty hadn't even done anything wrong. Who was this man who would hurt little boys for no reason other than pure meanness?

Little boys had a way of hurting themselves with no help from the trusted adults in their lives. We had our share of emergency room visits, usually involving Monty, because he was so fast and so inquisitive. He burned his hands on the kerosene heater because he ventured too close, and on the oven door as I opened it to extract our dinner. He busted his chin open when one foot slipped off the cement surrounding his grandma's pool and it had to be steri-stripped closed. But the first really bad injury came when Chad was 11 months old. He had been walking for about 3 months and still fell often but would always struggle back to his feet and move on. One afternoon I heard a quiet cry and peeked into the living room to see him lying face down on the floor. I cheerily said, "Hop up buddy!" and went on about my business. After a few seconds passed and he was still whimpering, I went to help him up. As I lifted him up to kiss away the tears, I quickly saw the reason he hadn't just hopped up. There was blood gushing from his eye. I could not see what he had done because there was too much blood. Luckily, we had phone service at that time and I quickly phoned my mother. She came to pick us up and rushed us to the emergency room. They would not let me stay in the operating room, as they tied my baby down and stitched his upper and lower eyelids back. They had both been split right up the middle when he had fallen into a wooden bookshelf that was attached to the wall. I had never felt so helpless as when I heard my baby screaming for me through the heavy metal doors that separated the operating room from the waiting room. It was torture for both he and I.

My days became consumed with the adventures of raising two babies. Our lives seemed pretty good. I adored my babies and for the most part it was the three of us. Every day was an adventure and there were days I wondered if the three of us would survive their childhood because of their antics. The setup of our trailer was not ideal for two exceptionally smart and perpetually active toddlers. In today's modern world I may have had alarms and baby monitors to assist me but even if those things were available, I couldn't have afforded them anyway. My bedroom was on one end of the 70-foot-long abode and theirs was on the opposite end. At night I would fall into my bed after a long day providing nourishment, guidance and protection for these two angels who had been entrusted to my care, and I would crash soundly into my pillow, dead to the world. This would have been ok if Monty liked to sleep as much as his brother did, but Monty's internal alarm clock didn't work that way. Monty didn't want to miss one second of each new day and was up with the sun. Not wanting his brother to miss out on anything either, he made sure that Chad was up with the sun too. It became routine for me to awaken with a start, jump from my bed to find that once again they had been up for some time making mischief. I smiled at the joyful giggles coming from the kitchen one summer morning until I rounded the corner to find the two of them sitting on the kitchen floor with my flour canister in between them. Apparently, they were missing the winter and had found an ingenious way to make it snow. As they scooped up handfuls of flour from the canister and threw it into the air, their laughter and tiny particles of the white stuff filled the air. The tiny particles of the white stuff filled every crack and crevice within 100 feet, but it sure seemed like fun to them. On another particularly inspired day, the two of them must have been feeling artistic as they retrieved sticks of margarine from the fridge and proceeded to paint their entire bedroom with them. They painted the walls, their beds and the carpet. If nothing else, the two tots were very thorough in their endeavors. The number for poison control was on speed dial, as I never knew when they might ingest such things as the remnants of a bottle of Children's Liquid Tylenol or some tasty kerosene and when Monty became tall enough to unlock the door, he began to also assist the neighbors with beginning their day early. On more than one occasion I found myself sitting on the floor, pulling my hair out. It is not always just a meaningless saying when someone states "I was about to pull my hair out." I know firsthand that sometimes it can be factual. When I would catch myself doing it, I would secretly wonder if I was losing my mind. My husband often would say I was crazy, maybe he was right, maybe it was me. But there was no time to think of it for long or my home may have come crashing down around me.

In my life, there was no down time and no time to be sick or injured so when my tooth began hurting, I tried to ignore it. When it got me down on the couch, my two toddlers were very helpful in retrieving the bottle of Tylenol from the bathroom and a glass of water from the kitchen. The pain was excruciating, and my face swelled up like a balloon. For once, I was anxiously awaiting my husband's return home because I needed help. I needed him to go somewhere and call for help. We were at one of those times when we had no phone and I needed a dentist desperately. When he finally arrived home, he was disinterested at best. He refused to call for help and stomped off to our bedroom closing himself off to the world and off to his family. I wondered if he even cared about me at all as I struggled to drag myself off the couch and out the door. As I began the walk, two doors down to my mother's house, I could barely keep my eyes open because of the pain. I clutched my face to relieve it, but nothing helped. My mother gasped in disbelief when she saw my distended face and I bitterly called the dentist myself. Speaking was excruciating. I had known for some time I was in this thing called life alone but feeling as though no one cares still hurt almost as much as the abscess in my mouth that was about to burst. After driving myself quickly to the dentist, I was told that had I waited any longer the infection was so bad I could have died. I slowly absorbed the reality that my 3-year-old son had more empathy for me than my husband did, and he didn't even understand how bad it was. He just knew that Mommy was sad and that made him sad and he wanted to help me. This was my reality and I slowly came to accept it.

Rather than focus on what was lacking, I filled my days with teaching my boys everything they needed to know about life. Monty learned to sight read and could accurately place the cards with names of all the items in our house correctly on them. Chad was struggling to talk. He had a lot to say but the words wouldn't come out very clear. He began getting frustrated if he couldn't get you to understand, and often would breakdown, crying in frustration. To avoid meltdowns, I would pretend I understood and just agree with him. Most of the time this worked. Chad was a very sensitive child, or as his dad would snarl, "A Mama's boy." This infuriated Brandon and Chad seemed to bear the brunt of his wrath because of this. Brandon viewed Chad's crying and clinginess to me as a weakness that must be corrected. By this time, the boys were getting regular whippings from their dad, but he only used his hand and I would qualify them as spankings. The problem was the length of them. He didn't just swat their bottoms and he didn't just spank them 2 or 3 times. He would begin spanking them and wouldn't stop until I stepped in and made him. This was a tough spot to be in. I had been raised that the father was the head of the household and had never once seen my mother contradict my father. I felt that a wife should honor and respect her husband and teach her children to do the same, yet, he was spanking them excessively. Over time I began thinking that maybe he was right. Maybe I was too soft. I didn't want my boys to grow up to be bad. I knew the Bible says "Spare the rod and spoil the child." It was so hard for me to sort it all out, but time and time again I found myself unable to bear the intensity of their spankings and would step in and pull them away from him. Chad's whippings were always worse than his brothers. Monty had a very high pain tolerance and would just take it like a little man, but Chad would cry out for me to save him and this provoked his father even more. Eventually I would convince him to stop the whipping and would comfort my boys and vow that tomorrow I would do a better job of keeping the kids out of his way. I also became an expert at hiding my situation to those on the outside.

Big brother Monty age 3 with his arm protectively around his little brother Chad age 1

My neighbor had become my best friend, but she never had a clue of what went on behind closed doors. No one did. We spent most days together at one trailer or the other and the kids seemed to enjoy playing together. I really began to see her as a trusted friend and so I was crushed on the day I returned home from the grocery with my two babies in tow and Brandon reported to me that my best friend, Sherri,

STACY MEHAFFEY

had propositioned him. He said she had come over as soon as she saw me leave for the grocery store and was hoping to have sex with him. He told me I should not be friends with her or talk to her ever again because she was bad news. I solemnly agreed but the next day just couldn't shake the feeling that something wasn't right. How could I have so grossly misjudged her character? I thought she was my friend. I cautiously ventured over to her trailer and confronted her. The look of fear in her eyes was difficult to read, something had happened, but her version of the events was way different from my husband's. She stated that he had come over and propositioned her as soon as I had left for the grocery and she had turned him down flat. So now I was faced with yet another difficult choice. I either believed my friend of a couple years or my husband whom I had devoted my life to and vowed to be with forever. The choice was easy. My husband must have been telling the truth. I loved him and would never dream of cheating on him, so he must feel the same way about our sacred bond. This is one of my many poor decisions that I struggle to understand. Why would I have thought he loved me? He had demonstrated quite the opposite, a seething hatred for me by the names he called me, and his blatant disregard for my well-being but, apparently, I disregarded those actions and chose to blindly believe his every word. Maybe it was more that I needed to believe what he said. Marriage was forever after all. What choice did I have, divorce? That was not an option. My parents would be so ashamed. The more tolerable option was to pretend that he loved me and that we were going to live happily ever after. I immediately ended my friendship with my only ally I had in the world, and once again became isolated. This time the aloneness was not due to distance or a guard dog, but by disconnectedness and mistrust.

I hardly had time to dwell on my loss of friendship with all that was going on at home anyway. The blow of Brandon quitting his job after Chad was born sucked us into a hole that we had not been able to climb out of. Brandon found work, but it was not quite the pay he had before, and the bills were mounting. We were so overextended before the drop in pay, and now it was simply impossible to pay for everything. As things began to close in on us, Brandon came up with a solution. We would leave all our troubles behind and move to sunny Florida. His parents had moved there, and his mother had been hounding us about keeping her grandbabies from her. I told him that I didn't think you could just run from your bills, and he explained that we would leave the trailer and the cars in Indiana. The bank would just come and pick them up and sell them to satisfy our loans. This didn't make sense to

64

me, but he wasn't asking for my opinion of the plan. We loaded up our two babies and fled to Florida, leaving our troubles and all our earthly belongings behind for the bank to repossess.

We arrived in Florida with two babies, no home and no job. Who needs a plan? We could just live on love, right? Well, maybe not. His parents were very accommodating and allowed us to move into their garage. I made the best of things and turned our little square abode into a home. Sectioning it off into four sections, each representing a different room. We had no bathroom and no running water, but I determined in my heart that this would be an adventure. My biggest problem now was how his mother treated us. She was always peeking in through the garage windows and going through our things when we were out. I thought she hated me. She didn't like that I always wanted to go to church and that I was not shy about making my opinions known. At times she would go into a rage and I could see a frightening visible change in her eyes. All these things led to me feeling a bit uneasy raising my babies in her garage.

To make matters worse, a new job never materialized. According to Brandon, there were so many snowbirds in Florida that wanted to work in machine shops as a hobby rather than to pay their bills, that no one wanted to pay him what he was worth. What was he worth? If our plight hadn't been so bleak, I may have chuckled at that looming question. As Brandon's dissatisfaction with himself rose, so did his insecurities. He began telling me that he was too good for me and about how worthless I was. I had a daily emotional beat down. He would quiz me about every boy I had ever dated and wanted to know exactly what happened on each and every date. He would then rage out of control about every one of them. One day out of desperation I told him, "I am who I am and if you are so unhappy with me, then maybe you should just go and find someone who can make you happy." I couldn't believe those words had come out of my mouth. I did not want a divorce. It was just a tactic to get him to stop the emotional abuse. It worked to some degree. The daily inquisitions stopped, but the degradations were a constant. Eventually he had to admit that this move was an utter failure. He couldn't find a job and we had sunk to a new all-time low. Eventually, we moved again, not just down the road mind you, but back across the 913 miles from whence we had come. All this moving around was wearing on me but at least we had downsized when we made the move to Florida, so we had very little to pack up.

Back in Indiana again, we were financially at rock bottom. I don't recall the amount of time he had been without a job, but we had nothing. We moved our little family into a duplex and our belongings were sparse at best. As Christmas was fast approaching, I realized that we were not going to be able to rob Peter to pay Paul this year. In the past, we had just always taken the last paycheck before Christmas, said screw it to the bill collectors, and bought Christmas. No one is going to turn out your lights at Christmas, right? But this year even Peter was broke. There was no paycheck to steal from. I looked at my two wide eyed innocent boys who believed that Santa was coming and feared that a little more of their childhood was about to be stolen from them. The feeling was a new low for me. Then we received a miracle in the form of my brother. I don't know how he knew, but he showed up at our house on Christmas eve with $60 in hand. He wanted to be sure the boys had Christmas. I didn't even mind the Christmas Eve rush that year, as I hurried to pick up some gifts for my babies. After putting gas in the car and buying groceries there was just enough left to have a splendid Christmas. I remember being amazed that they loved their little bucket of army men so much. Even if you don't have that much money, you can still have a good Christmas, and I was so thankful for what we had been given.

Brandon, however, never seemed to be thankful for anything. He and I were fighting a lot in those days and it was in this house that he first put his hands on me in anger. We had been arguing about something and he had decided to claim his wife afterwards. For the first time, I refused him. I was tired of him treating me so badly with no repercussions. The cycle was very clear. He would blow up yelling, screaming and breaking things then would want to make up and reclaim his wife. Well I wasn't in the mood, so I said no. It didn't matter what I did or didn't want, it never really did with him, and I guess I should have foreseen what was coming. He was very strong and I, at 118 pounds, was no match for his muscle-bound male body. He held me down and took what he deemed his. Hysterically I struggled to get away, to no avail. When he finally finished, I tore myself away and through my tears grabbed my boys and ran from the house. I was done. I would not stay with a man who would force himself on me. Why should I? He had already proven that he didn't love me. I tore off in the car and vowed to never go back again. I instinctively headed toward the house of my childhood. At one time, it had been my safe harbor. As I approached my parent's home, I remembered my mother's words, "Don't tell me about your marital problems." My heart sank as I realized I couldn't go there. I surveyed my options. There were none. I no longer had any friends and my parents had made their position known. My resolve began to weaken. What was I thinking anyway? Divorce was wrong. I would be letting everyone down again if I got a divorce. My parents would be devastated, and I had caused them enough pain. Besides all of that, I had two babies to think of now. Who was I to take their daddy away from them? I drove that long country road as slow as I could and returned home wholeheartedly defeated. I resigned myself to live out the commitment I had made before God to my marriage...no matter how miserable it was.

After returning home, it was back to life as usual. There was never any apology. Brandon would simply go back to acting as though nothing had happened. He began talking about another baby. Maybe we could have a little girl. It would be nice to have another girl amongst of all these boys. I know it seems crazy to even contemplate bringing in another innocent child into this fiasco, but I had returned home with the mindset that I was going to make this work. I threw myself into my marriage once again with absolute conviction. I think I was living in denial. I didn't see things as they really were. I knew Brandon was not happy. In fact, he was downright angry, but I just needed to prove to him that I loved him. I needed to reassure him that he had nothing to fear. I could surely do that. After all, wasn't his aggression toward me all based on fear? If I could do a better job of making him feel secure, then I could make things change. His anger toward the kids however, I didn't understand. Maybe I was just overprotective. Maybe I was trying to raise a couple of sissy boys. Children needed to behave. If I hadn't been so soft on them, they probably wouldn't be mischievous. If I were a better mother, they would toe the line and then he wouldn't lose his temper. Nonetheless, I would need to do a better job of keeping them out of his way.

I was afraid to leave my children alone with their father, so everywhere I went, the boys went as well, and our shopping trips were inevitably eventful. On one particularly trying day, the boys were being extra naughty and we had forged our way through only about half of the store when I turned to see the two of them in a full-on knockdown, drag out wrestling match on the disgustingly dirty floor of the grocery store. It was more than I could endure and through tears I escorted two shocked little boys out to the car, leaving my half full grocery cart in the middle of the aisle. Shopping it seemed was not something to be enjoyed even on the rare occasion that it meant having another adult along for the ride. That same year my cousin

Becky and I were in charge of planning the annual Mother-Daughter banquet for the church that year, so we decided on a full day of shopping to purchase the supplies. Although it was always fun to hang out with Becky, shopping with two rambunctious boys was not so much. After a long, exhausting day, we finally finished up with Mr. Super-Rent being our final stop and had wearily begun the 30-minute drive toward home. I sunk back deeper into the inviting plush seat of her car, closing my eyes and listening to the friendly chatter coming from my boys in the back seat. When they weren't fighting, they were the best of friends. As I floated closer and closer to a peaceful sleep, I was jolted back to reality by a huge gasp from the younger of the two. I strained to hear the conversation and learned that Monty had just revealed to his brother that he had taken something from the last store we had been at. When I demanded to see what he had taken, he remorsefully produced a 25¢ pencil. I breathed in deeply and shot a knowing glance over at my equally exhausted companion. She asked, "What do you want to do?" as if I really had a choice. I wanted to be magically whisked away to a peaceful beach somewhere, basking in the warm sun with the only sound being the sound of the waves hitting the shoreline and the gentle ocean breeze blowing through my hair, but instead I was here. In a little red Chevy Chevette, preparing to lengthen our already exhausting day by doing the right thing. As we turned around and headed back across town, I pondered silently as to how this should be handled. As it turned out, Chad was a great help with this endeavor as he wailed with remorse and tearfully inquired as to whether they would put his brother in jail. He woefully fretted about how long they would have to be apart and if the handcuffs would hurt. With my back to them, neither boy could see the smile that was threatening to creep across my face. No lecture was needed at this time. Chad was handling this situation perfectly. By the time we reached the store Monty was thoroughly terror stricken at the prospect of never seeing his family again. I explained to him, that he would have to confess his transgression to the clerk and hope for mercy from her. He slowly shuffled back into the store with his head and shoulders slumped so low to the ground that I thought he might fall. As we re-entered the store, I have no doubt the clerk remembered us and gave me an inquiring look. I explained that Monty had something to tell her and she looked inquisitively back to him. He quietly explained that he had stolen a pencil and was returning it and how sorry he was for doing such a bad thing. Expecting a little support from this adult, I was stunned when all she could say in response was, "Are you kidding me? All he took was a pencil and you made him return it?"

I thanked her sarcastically for her support and quickly exited the store before his offense could be further minimized. I could only hope that his worried brother's words would linger longer than the unconcerned clerk's. One thing was evident, I had both hands full with these two rambunctious boys.

6

LOST HOPE

Wrangling 2 busy boys and attempting to keep their father happy was enough to keep me more than busy. Even with everything I was dealing with, approximately 9 months later, another responsibility was given to me in the form of a precious baby girl.

Whitney was an absolute angel, a beautiful little princess. I finally had my little girl. I refused to dress her in any blue. Everything had to be pink. As we were just getting settled in with our little family of 5, we moved again. All the way back to Florida. This time we were not close to his parents, we were in a little town called Webster. It was not a tropical paradise, central Florida is rather ugly, but we made the best of it. I was so lonely. I had no friends and no life other than caring for my children. I became friends with our Mexican neighbors. They spoke broken English and were in awe of Whitney's "golden hair." I learned that extended families could all live under one roof and that everything could be placed in a tortilla and eaten like a burrito, even Spam. I guess three kids can keep you busy enough that you don't have time for friends anyway, but I felt extremely alone.

I was so happy the day a saw a man with a Bible approaching my front door. I eagerly let him in as he smiled and talked to me about God and his love and peace on earth. I almost felt like I was back home at the little Baptist church again and warm feelings began to flood over my body. He then went on to talk about heaven on earth and earning your way to heaven and things began feeling not so right. I had nothing else to do, so I debated the differences between the way I had been raised and what he believed and found that I really lacked the knowledge to make a good argument for what I believed. As a child when I had questioned our beliefs, I had always been shamed and told that it was so because the Bible said it was so. This argument may somewhat satisfy a child, but it wasn't satisfying this grown man who was arguing otherwise, and I found that it wasn't really satisfying me either. I stuck to my guns however and the meeting ended badly. He became offended when I told him I would allow him to leave his literature so that he would not lead another poor innocent soul astray and I tossed it into the trash as he stomped angrily down the sidewalk to continue his mission to convert the world.

This did get me thinking for the first time in my life about why I believed what I believed. I knew there was a God who sent His son Jesus to die on the cross for our sins. We were all basically bad people who didn't deserve to go to heaven, but because of Jesus paying the price for our sins we had a way into heaven. I believed that but why did I believe it? I guess because that is what I had always been told, just as that man believed what he had always been taught. I wondered; how could one know what was right? There were so many different religions in the world, and I was certain that each and every one believed their way was the right way. Growing up, I was taught that the Separate Baptist way was the only way, all the other religions were wrong. The Methodists were disrespectful in the way they dressed in church and the Christian church believed in eternal salvation meaning once saved always saved. It was explained to me that this meant they thought that they could go around sinning with no consequence just because they had asked Jesus into their heart. Then there were the Catholics. I had been taught, they didn't even worship God. They worshiped Mary. Obviously, there was only one true way and that was the Separate Baptist way. For the first time in my life, I began to question what I had been told. Maybe the way I had always been taught was not true. I had never really been given a rational reason why it was true. This began the wheels turning in my head and I began a quest to discover who God was for myself. With a baby girl and two active boys there was little time to do much soul searching. But one thing

I knew. God was always there. He was there watching over my precious babies and making sure they had the things they needed.

This was the case when Whitney was coming of age to begin walking. Money was tight, as always, and we had no way to purchase a pair of shoes for her. At this time, it was expected that as your child reached an age where she was attempting to walk, you would purchase what were called walking shoes. They were white leather high top shoes that laced up the front and had a wide, flat bottom to help with balance. They could only be found at Buster Brown shoe store, which was out of my league for sure. As lottery tickets are the poor man's hope for an escape, much to my chagrin, Brandon purchased one at a local gas station. I scratched it off in the car and we had won $40. That would be enough to buy our baby her first shoes. I never considered whether it was luck or divine intervention. I was just so relieved that we could get her what she needed.

By Whitney's first birthday we were back in Indiana again. I was so weary of moving my family across the country. Monty was getting close to school age and I wanted to put down some roots. I didn't want him to be constantly ripped from one school to another and though very out of character for me, I demanded that the moving our family back and forth cease. I explained my concern to Brandon and he pretended to listen. The only house we could find that was in our budget should have been condemned. The first time I saw it, I was appalled. There was no way we could make this work. But after a couple of weeks of looking for a better home within our price range, I finally conceded. I would accept the challenge of turning this dilapidated old farmhouse into a home. One by one, I turned each room into our home. I painted and wallpapered and added all the little touches that make a house a home. I decorated Monty's room in horses, Chad's in trains and Whitney's in clowns as I tried desperately to make my children's lives have some semblance of fun. I skillfully hid our family secret from the outside world, and no one knew of the ever-escalating abuse that was going on within the walls of our home.

As it turned out, that house held many fun memories for us. It was where Monty learned to ride his bike and the boys got to explore the barn and fields tirelessly. I took them fishing at the pond down the road and taught them how to throw and catch a baseball for tee-ball. No matter how long I practiced with them, it was never enough for Chad. He would spend hours after Monty, Whitney and I had gone inside, throwing the baseball against the propane tank in the front yard, playing catch with himself. He spent so much time that summer doing it that he had a most strange tan line on his hand from the baseball glove.

Everything was not fun and games though, and my children's propensity for mischief didn't stop, that is for sure. If I ever turned my head for a moment, they were up to something. Monty coated Whitney's hair with Vaseline one afternoon, which by the way is nearly impossible to get out. After several washings, she still looked like a greaser. I walked into the bathroom another day to find both boys using my tampons for rocket ships as they pushed their fingers up through the bottom and yelled, "Blast off." While these things were aggravating, they truly were harmless but some of their antics were a little more serious as I would learn one beautiful Sunday evening

As we were headed to the annual Bible school program, Whitney began violently throwing up. The vomit was everywhere, from her tiny lavender bow on her head, to her ruffles on her little dress, all the way down to the ruffles on her little socks. I was so disappointed that she was getting sick. We were so looking forward to church that evening but if she were sick, we couldn't go. I dismally turned the car back toward home as the vomiting continued. I didn't understand how this had come on so quickly. She hadn't given any indication that she was coming down with something. As we pulled into the drive the guilt overtook Monty and he confessed. He and Chad had fed her poison. Aghast, I inquired as to what kind of poison. He informed me that it was made up of a little bit of everything that could be found underneath the bathroom cabinet. They had formulated a poison from mixing them all together and then offered it to their 2-year-old sister to try. Lucky for me, I knew the number for poison control and was able to call quickly. They assured me that since she was already throwing up, her body was getting rid of the toxin naturally and all I need do was to watch her.

The danger was not limited to the little one in the family. On yet another exciting day in my household, I walked into the bathroom to find the boys had filled up the sink with water, wrapped a washcloth around my curling iron, which was plugged in, and were holding the metal barrel with both hands while immersing the entire thing into the sink full of water. They giggled as the electricity flowed into their little hands and up their arms and I once again, wondered if we would all survive until they were grown. In hindsight, I should have placed a lock on that bathroom door as that seemed to be where they found most of their danger, but I didn't think of it at the time. I guess I was just too busy trying to keep up. On another day, Monty somehow got Whitney out into the back yard without my knowledge. He had let the garden hose run for some time and it had resulted in quite the glorious mud pit forming alongside the house. I am certain he was only practicing his skills giving mud baths and concerned with the health of her joints and skin but once again, poor little Whitney was the target of his experiment. I missed her presence just in time to find him putting the finishing touches on his work and to find her covered from head to toe with brown mud. They were both covered as he let her practice her skills on him as well. Although probably the wrong thing to do, I quickly ran back inside to retrieve the camera before using the garden hose to spray them off. Whitney was quite the prissy girl and loved to strut around in dresses, wearing bracelets and rings and carrying a purse. One day I overheard the boys planning a mugging. Monty was to stand on one side of the doorway and Chad on the other and as Whitney came through the door, one would grab her and the other would grab her purse and steal it. I wondered how she would handle it and rather than intervene immediately, I sat back to discreetly watch the scene unfold. The boys obviously got more than they had anticipated from their rambunctious little sister as she let out a war cry that startled all three of us and began chasing them through the house with her purse flying high over her head and landing repeatedly on theirs. I was proud of the little thing for being able to handle herself. Maybe having two big brothers would have some benefit for her. She had learned to hold her own.

There are several pivotal moments in a person's life, and one was about to occur in mine. I had taken Monty to be tested for Kindergarten placement at Union, the same school I had attended, and he did fabulously. Under my careful guidance he had excelled, and I often wondered if I had a little genius on my hands. He was so smart. I could hardly wait to share him with the world. As Monty was preparing to begin Kindergarten, Brandon returned from work one day to announce that he was moving back to Florida. He added, "If you want to come great, if you don't, then have a nice life." I was stunned. Did he not care if his family came with him? I was crushed as his actions proved once again that he really didn't love me. I felt strongly that Monty shouldn't be taken out of school but had always been taught that the husband was the head of the household. This obviously was not up for discussion with him. His decision had been made and now the ball was in my court. I felt that at the very least, the kids deserved to have a father in their lives and resolved in my heart to go but I was torn. I didn't want to go. I began constantly praying about this decision. One night as I lay in bed praying about my dilemma, I heard a strong and distinct voice say, "You are doing my will. Go with your husband." As I opened my eyes and looked up, I saw a figure hovering above our bed. I was frozen in fear. My heart was pounding out of my chest. I felt as though I couldn't breath and I wanted to wake my husband but was paralyzed by fear. I struggled to interpret what I was seeing. I briefly wondered if it were a demon but the glow that surrounded it seemed so peaceful and serene. I strained my eyes to get a better look and as quickly as it came, it was gone. I lay in bed as my heart rate slowly returned to normal and contemplated what had just happened. Had God just spoken to me or sent an angel to speak to me? I hardly seemed important enough to get that kind of attention. God sent angels to speak to important people like the mother of Jesus, not lowly losers like me. Maybe God did still care about me even though I had made a terrible mess of things. One thing was certain, the voice had said I was to go with my husband. I resolved in my heart to make that horrendous move once again.

Monty age 7, Chad age 5, and Whitney age 3

By the time school started in the fall, we had moved into a home in Rainbow Lakes Estates. Don't let the name fool you. There was really nothing estate-like about it. It was full of moderate to low-income homes but, as always, I sucked it up and we lived like life was good. Most of the time it was. We only had the occasional outburst from Brandon when I failed to keep the kids from underfoot. They were smart and I was good, so the eruptions happened maybe once every two weeks and were fairly short lived. The problem was, as the boys grew bigger, Brandon grew more violent and what once was extensive whippings with his hands had turned to whippings with a belt and eventually into closed fist punches. Every time I vowed to do a better job and wondered how long it would take me to master this wife and motherhood thing. The overlying feeling was one of living on eggshells. Tension hung in the air whenever Brandon was home. The mood in our home would begin to change as I anticipated his return. I would frantically begin making sure the house was in order and try to usher the children to their rooms with instructions to keep their voices quiet so as not to upset their dad. Luckily, he wasn't around all that much, so it wasn't too hard to pretend that life was good. Most of the time for the kids and me it was.

The big day finally arrived. I set my alarm to awaken in time to fix Monty breakfast and get him ready for his first day of school. As I stumbled out of bed and to my bedroom door, I was shocked to find my five-year-old fully dressed, with his backpack on his back and waiting on the other side of the door with the biggest smile imaginable. He was so innocent and full of excitement to begin school. Little did he or I know what was to come. Neither of us realized that precocious children with an overabundance of energy really did not fit in well in the normal school setting. I naively couldn't wait to share my little genius with the world. He had been advanced developmentally his entire life, but somehow, school for Monty would always be a struggle. My first sign of trouble came early on when he got off the school bus crying. When I inquired as to what was going on, he told a heartbreaking tale of a bully on the bus who everyday would demand to see Monty's lunch. When Monty would open it up, the bully would begin taunting him and tell him that his mother could not possibly love him, or I would pack him a better lunch. My first instinct was to climb up on that school bus the next morning and have a talk with that vile child and inattentive bus driver that would make their heads spin, but then as I calmed down I reasoned that I would really be doing Monty no favors in fighting his battles for him. He should learn to fight his own battles and it was my responsibility to provide him with the skills to do so. I told him that he did not have to show the boy his lunch. This was news to him, and he smiled as I told him that tomorrow when the bully asked to see his lunch he was to say "no." The next morning came way too early and I struggled to follow through with this first step into independence for my first-born son. At five, was he big enough to begin fighting his own battles? I held my breath through the day and anxiously awaited the roar of the bus signaling his return. I met him in the driveway and immediately noticed his face was red but had a huge smile on it. As I inquired as to the events of the day, he informed me that he did not show the bully what was in his lunch box. When the boy had demanded it and Monty refused, the ruffian punched my baby in the face knocking him to the floor of the bus. I gasped in horror and I inquired as to why he was smiling about that. He proudly retorted that he was smiling because it didn't even hurt, and he had jumped up and punched the boy back and sent him running back to his seat crying. The boy would never approach Monty again. I am sure he found an easier target that wouldn't fight back, but Monty had learned not to be a victim. He had learned it was ok to stand up for yourself. I find this interesting looking back, that I was able to teach my child a lesson that I was unable to implement in my own life.

Life for me was once again lonely. I wasn't allowed to work or venture outside the home on my own, so I had no colleagues. I had no friends except when a neighbor needed a babysitter. I went to church weekly, but I remember feeling like such an outsider. I saw all these perfect people with their perfect lives and then there was me. I wasn't like these people. My husband wouldn't even attend church with me. I didn't have the fancy clothes and shoes like they did and to hear them talk, their lives were perfect as well. I remember wishing just one of them would have a flaw, a little crack in that shell of perfection so that I would have a way in. But if there was one, I couldn't see it. So, I sat in church week after week isolated and alone. Finally, I was invited to a jewelry party by one of the ladies in my Sunday School class. I was so excited to be part of something at last. But the party wasn't what I had expected. I am sure the ladies were nice enough but after I got one look at the prices of the jewelry, my mind could think of nothing else. I couldn't afford this extravagance. I couldn't even afford food for the week and now I was expected to buy an overpriced bauble. I had to purchase something. I would look like a freeloader if I came to the party only to eat their food and didn't buy anything. I spent the next hour flipping repeatedly through the book to find the cheapest item. I felt nauseous at the thought of what I was about to do but felt as though I had no choice. I purchased the cheapest item and my bill came to $27.52. I wrote the check out and headed for my car with tears in my eyes. That was a foolish thing to do. I should have never thought I could be a friend with these perfect, rich people. How could I justify this irresponsible purchase of a non-essential item like jewelry, when I didn't even know if we would have food for all seven days of the next week? By the time I reached home, I was so overcome with regret that I made the dreaded phone call and disgracefully asked the woman from church to please cancel my order. How would I ever face these women at church again after doing such a dreadful thing? Surely, they would all be talking about me and looking down on me.

I became even more isolated, although whether by my own doing or by my husband's design I can't know for sure. We stayed in Rainbow Lakes Estates for some time and eventually the boys met a couple of neighbors by riding their bikes past their house. They introduced us and these two would become my first real friends in Florida. These two women may have known a bit about feeling unaccepted as they had an unconventional relationship that was not at this time accepted by society. But they were kind to me. They wanted to talk to me, to see how my day was going, not to see what they could get from me. They often invited the kids and me to go to the lake and ride on their boat and Jet Ski. During this time, they were my one connection to the outside world but even they didn't know our secret. I threw myself into being the best mom and wife ever. I tried to make every day an adventure and have many fond memories of our days together. We would have picnics in the back yard and scavenger hunts to try and make every day exciting.

In those days, even without trying, life seemed to offer one adventure after another and early one morning, as I loaded the children up in the car to begin our trek to school, it began pouring down rain. It wasn't just sprinkling a little, rather it was more like a monsoon and I could see nothing. The line down the middle of the road was not visible, nor were the sides of the road. Luckily, I pulled out onto the main highway behind a car and could use her lights to guide me. I was following entirely too closely, because if I got back to a safe distance her lights would disappear into a veil of rain. My hands gripped the steering wheel as I leaned forward in senior citizen fashion and strained to see the road before me. As I desperately tried to keep her taillights in view, suddenly her taillights began to slowly spin sideways, and I immediately realized she had begun to hydroplane and was no longer in control of her vehicle. There was no time to react as I watched her spin into oncoming traffic head on, collide with an unsuspecting motorist and then come directly back toward me. I instructed the kids to hold on as we braced for the impending impact. I held my breath as 3500 pounds of steel came barreling toward the front of my vehicle, which was carrying the most precious of all my possessions. At the exact moment when the impact should have occurred, there was a flash of light and my car floated through the scene of the accident untouched and we glided to an uneventful stop on the side of the road. Confused and scared I briefly attempted to calm my hysterical kids and instructed them to not move from their seat belts. I jumped from the car and ran through the downpour to check on the drivers of the other two vehicles. We were on a long stretch of highway with nothing around and there were no other vehicles or houses nearby. The passengers of the cars were injured but not critically and after several minutes, an emergency crew arrived relieving me of my nursing duties. As I remembered my frightened children, I ran franticly back to the car expecting to return to inconsolable crying, but they were perfectly calm. When I questioned this, they told me that they had been scared and crying but the man told them not to be afraid. He said that everything would be ok. I looked around and there was nothing near, no houses, no other cars, nothing. The only people on that road had been the three cars involved in the accident and no one from any of those included a man able to walk around. I inquired further as to what he looked like and they told me a man in white came over to the driver's side window and spoke to them saying, "Don't be afraid. Everything will be alright." It was a torrential down pour outside, with the rain beating down loudly yet they were able to hear a man speaking to them from outside the car with all of the windows rolled up? Tears began to form in my eyes, as I realized the magnitude of what had just happened. I began piecing the story together in my mind. Why had we not crashed into the oncoming car spinning out of control? What was that flash of light when there should have been a head on collision? Who was the mysterious man in white comforting my children? Where had he come from and where had he gone? Had we just seen an angel?

My life pin-balled back and forth from the supernatural to the super mundane it seemed. I knew God was out there by the way He showed himself to me in the most tumultuous times of my life, but where was He in my day to day? The bills piled up and we ran again but this time it was only a few towns over. We never had any money. Brandon was working with his dad and brother in the family business but claimed they weren't paying him fairly. The auto auctions kept him away from home until the wee hours of the morning. Had I sensed any impropriety, I could have easily found out the truth about his whereabouts, but I either didn't suspect or wouldn't allow my mind to go there. So, I lived my life in ignorant bliss struggling to feed my three kids while my husband was gallivanting with other women and spending our money on beer and entertainment for them. Perhaps I didn't see what was going on because I was just thankful that he wasn't around. Our house was much more peaceful when it was just the kids and me. Most evenings, I was already asleep when he arrived home. Those were the best nights because there would be no outbursts or beatings to break up. It was about this time in my life, when I started feeling like I had sat by and let us sink deeper and deeper into debt and despair long enough. I briefly entertained thoughts of getting a job to help with the money situation. If nothing else, maybe I could buy us food, but Brandon adamantly disagreed. Any thoughts of working outside of the home were quickly squashed and I dejectedly resigned myself to being a stay at home mom. Maybe Brandon was right. Maybe my place was at home with the kids. I was the only one that could be trusted to take care of them anyway. I don't know what I was thinking. Money became tighter and tighter and weeks would pass by with no grocery money. Our food supply dwindled, and my meals were no longer carefully planned to include the four food groups, rather they were planned to make the most out of the meager contents of my pantry. Peanut butter became a staple and there were weeks when that was eaten every day. I tried to become creative by toasting it one day and having it on soft bread the next but peanut butter becomes very tiresome day after day. Other days, a can of green beans would feed myself and my three children. I remember those tasting like the best green beans I had ever eaten. Another meal was naked spaghetti noodles, which are not as bad as they sound if you add a little salt. The kids would complain about the food, but at least we had something to fill their little bellies. Well, at least most of the time we did. One day, I had totally exhausted all of our resources and there was nothing in the house to prepare for dinner. I desperately searched the couch cushions and the car seats for any spare change that could be used to purchase something at the grocery store. When my search was complete, I had found 68¢. It wasn't much but perhaps I could buy a loaf of bread or a can of green beans. As my children and I walked up and down every aisle of the store I realized that there was nothing that would feed my family for 68¢. As we made our way past the bakery the angel behind the counter offered the children a free cookie. They hungrily wolfed them down and we returned home with no dinner. I had failed once again.

I didn't like the feeling of being a failure, so I determined to find a way to provide for our family what my husband was not. I finally came up with a solution that would allow me to be there for my children but still earn an income. I started a day-care in my home. As word got out, we had a steady stream of extra children in our home. The first was a beautiful two-year-old little girl Mya, who was being raised by her grandmother. Her mother had a new boyfriend and no longer wanted to be burdened with a small child. This was probably in Mya's best interest because on the rare occasion her mother would take her home, she would come back with un-explained bruising, one time in the unmistakable shape of a hand. Her grandmother was resentful of the added responsibilities of raising Mya. When tax time rolled around the child's biological mother claimed her on her taxes and the grandmother found out. In what seemed like retaliation, she refused to pick the child up from my house the entire weekend stating that she was done raising Mya. She would call CPS on Monday to come and pick up this precious little girl. I was devastated and did not want that to happen. I volunteered to keep her. At least then she would be with people she knew instead of total strangers. In the end, the grandmother caved in and begrudgingly came to pick her up.

The second child I began watching was named Zoe. She was 18 months old and her mom and dad were having marital problems. When she first started coming, they were still living together, but not happily. They soon divorced and both became heavy drinkers. Dad disappeared from her life and on a Friday night, I could be fairly certain that neither would show to pick up their child. I never got a call, just an unfeeling, detached statement the following day when mom awoke from her stupor from a wild night of partying, that she had decided to go out the night before. It broke my heart as this baby figured out the drill and would begin sobbing when I pulled her pajamas out of her bag. She knew this meant her mommy wasn't coming to get her that night. One weekend was different though. I was told that her daddy would be picking her up after work. I was so happy for Zoe. She would get to spend the weekend with her daddy. She must wonder where he had gone. He arrived right on time to pick her up and after a weekend with her father, he dropped her off Monday morning again to me. But something was different.

When I attempted to remove her pants to change her diaper she began screaming hysterically. She had never acted that way before. In horror, I examined her more closely and though I had no experience in this area, her little body left no question as to what had happened over the weekend while in the care of her father. A sickening feeling washed over me. How could anyone be this depraved? She was a baby. I cautiously broached this sensitive subject with her mother that evening when she arrived to pick Zoe up and naively believed she would take care of things. I now know I should have called child protective services to report it but at the time, I didn't know there was such a service. Shortly after that they moved away. I never heard the rest of the story and I will forever wonder what became of little Zoe. I was dumbfounded by the revelation of evil in this world. There were many other children in and out of my home over the next couple of years, each with their own unfortunate story. They were teaching me about the real world out there. The world was entirely different from the safe and sheltered world I had grown up in. How could so many people be so uncaring and hurt their innocent children? It seemed as though something was missing in their hearts. I wanted to save them all. I wanted to rescue them and give them a chance in life. Strangely enough, I couldn't see that we too needed rescuing. I don't understand it to this day. Maybe I thought I was trying to fix our life and was being proactive about making things right. The abuse had gotten less frequent, as we all became more adept at staying out of Brandon's way, on the rare occasion he made his way home. The money I made at least insured that we always had food to eat.

Besides my skill at rationalizing my situation, another thing that quickly pushed any thoughts of making a change was quickly interrupted by the shenanigans of my two school age boys. One day I overheard them complaining about how mean and unfair their bus driver was. I smiled to myself, remembering my battles with heartless adults when I was in school and realized that I had survived it all. At the end of their complaint session they brightly came up with a solution. They would get kicked off the bus. Once that happened, their mother would drive them to school and they would never have to see that brutal bus driver again. Without thinking it through, I interjected that things didn't work that way in our house. I informed them that if they got kicked off the bus, as punishment for misbehaving, then they would be walking the three miles to school. To my disbelief, they came in from the bus the following day with discipline referrals, which stated that they were both kicked off the bus for three days. My heart sank as I realized that my threat had not been incentive enough to make them do the right thing. I now found myself in a quandary. If I did not do what I said I would do, then they would not believe me in the future. I made a mental note to myself, "Never make a threat you are unwilling to follow through with." Even though they were old enough and strong enough to walk three miles without any harm coming to them, that Florida highway was a scary place for two young boys without supervision, so I determined that I would have to follow behind them in my car. For the next three days I dragged poor Whitney up out of bed, strapped her into her car seat and we drove the three miles to school behind two little boys that were hopefully learning a lesson about believing their mother when she tells them something. The first day I sincerely wondered about the wisdom of my choice in punishments. The only ones who seemed unhappy about the walk to school were Whitney and me. The boys, with their backpacks strapped to their backs, were laughing and joking the entire way to the school. But the trek back home was not quite as jovial as they were tired from a long day at school. With each passing day, the novelty of the walk to school wore off and became the burden I had hoped and I began to think that this might actually produce the results I had originally designed it to produce. We had the occasional passerby stop and inquire if everything was ok and my explanation was met with mixed reviews. There were those, usually of the older generation who smiled knowingly and thanked me for trying to raise my children with a little respect for authority and others who would look at me with contempt as though I were abusing my children. How was I to know if I was doing the right thing? I had never raised kids before and I was virtually doing this on my own with no support. As their school bus would pass every day, I wondered what was going through that bus drivers mind. Was she as mean and heartless as they claimed, or did she feel a twinge of guilt every time she saw the results of her punishment? I will never know the answer to that, but I can tell you that someone was affected by it, because that was the one and only time those two got kicked off of a school bus.

As the bills piled up and the landlord got tired of not getting his rent, we were forced to move again, moving the kids to yet another school. I had given up on fighting to keep them in one school. It was a waste of time. Brandon didn't care about anyone but himself so when the bills would pile up and the heat became too much to bear, we would just pack up and move. Money was a constant concern for us as we never had any. Brandon had gone back to bringing home only $150 per week and I finally asked him to quit working for his family. I had done the math and he could bring home $206 a week working at McDonalds for minimum wage and only be gone for 40 hours, rather than the 80 he was putting in at the family business. He constantly complained that they didn't pay him as much as they brought home because, he claimed, he wasn't there when they initially started the business. He would not go for it saying that there is no way he could work for a boss. Having someone tell him what to do, was more than he could handle. As I resigned myself to living in poverty, my respect for this so-called man of the house fell to an all-time low. He didn't want me to work but he wasn't getting the job done. Frustrated, I dropped the issue so as not to set him off. The move seemed to always mean a new school and new friends for the kids. Monty never complained and Whitney loved the adventure of it, but Chad didn't. He hated change. While at this house we got a border collie puppy. Her name was Sox and she was a very smart dog. She had a litter of puppies a year later and was unable to feed them all because there were not enough places for them all to feed at once. There was one little runt who always seemed to get pushed away and by the time he could get to eat, the milk was all gone. I watched helplessly as all his brothers and sisters got bigger and stronger and he got weaker and smaller. I worried that this little fella would not make it. Then my fears were seemingly confirmed as Sox picked him up and left him alone behind a bush in our front yard, away from the rest of the litter. I was disappointed in her. I know that animals often can tell when one of their young is not going to make it and will abandon them, but I thought she was more human than that. As I watched in amazement, I realized that Sox wasn't abandoning that scrawny runt, she was saving his life. She would go out and lay behind the bush allowing him to feed first before all his greedy siblings and then she would let the rest of them eat. I was so proud of her for being such a good mama. The little runt quickly gained weight and strength and soon could hold his own.

While my dog seemed to have an extraordinary ability to be a good mom, I frequently felt like I was failing. I know that I gave my children love and fun adventures but as a mother, you want to give them everything and one thing they never got was dinner out at a restaurant. That was an extravagance we just could not afford. One day, with the money I had earned from baby-sitting, I decided to take the kids out to eat at McDonalds. We never went out to eat and I did it just because I wanted to. It was a very careless thing to do and quite out of character for me but, for whatever reason, I announced to my children that we were going out for dinner. I loaded them all up in the minivan and we headed downtown to the local McDonalds. Monty ordered his meal first, then Chad, then Whitney. I began to feel flush as I quickly did the math in my head. I hadn't realized how much this was going to cost. What had I been thinking? I ordered the cheapest hamburger on the menu to try to minimize the damage, but when the teenage girl behind the register announced my total to be $19.85, I suddenly lost my appetite. When did McDonalds become so expensive? I didn't have twenty extra dollars laying around to throw away on fast food. This was a mistake. I should never have brought my children here. I briefly considered cancelling right then and there but as I looked around at the joy I saw on my baby's faces, I just couldn't. We would just have to get by on a few less groceries this week. We had done it before. They were so looking forward to this special treat. We grabbed a booth to get the most out of our rare dining out experience and I tried to push this extravagant expense out of my mind and just enjoy my children, but my mind kept calculating and replaying the scene over and over, "That will be $19.85 ma'am." What a stupid, irresponsible adult I had been. We couldn't afford this. I needed to be better prepared so I wasn't blindsided in the future.

7

LOST DREAMS

t was around this time that I began thinking about preparing for my family's future. Brandon had been diagnosed with juvenile diabetes at the age of seven. Other than the daily insulin shots he took regularly, and the occasional after meal insulin, you would never know he had an incurable medical condition. Even though his body was not yet showing any evidence of the disease, my mother's words echoed in my head that if I married someone who had diabetes, that I would be left alone in life when he died an early death. At the time, her warning had seemed so cruel. But now, it was a reality I was living with. What would I do if something happened to him? Other than baby-sitting, I hadn't had a job in my life, and I had three children to provide for. Divorce was nowhere in my mind at this time, but I think God sees all and was preparing me for what was to come. Whitney was getting ready to begin kindergarten and I had always thought in the back of my mind, that when my kids were all in school, I would go back to school. I anxiously signed up for college placement testing at the local college. High school seemed like so long ago. I wondered if I would remember anything. Brandon thought it was a bad idea, but, on this, I stood my ground. I had to be sure of a future for my children should something happen to their father. It was my duty as their parent to be sure they were provided for. It now seems so contradictory that we often had no food and they were in constant fear of abuse, but I was determined to ensure future income.

On the morning before I was to go for testing I was feeling particularly chipper at the new prospects that lay in front of me and as I returned from walking the boys down our long lane to the bus, I was being a bit goofy and not paying close attention to the terrain. As I danced and skipped my way back to the house singing all the way, my foot landed halfway in a large hole in the yard and down I went. As that all too familiar pain that comes along with a broken bone shot up through my calf, I struggled to get back up on my feet. Try as I might, it wasn't happening. I thought back to the many sprained ankles I had endured during my high school years of basketball and, although painful, I was always able to immediately limp on those. I finally gave up on standing and crawled the rest of the way into the house. My thoughts raced as I pondered how I was going to manage to get ready, take care of Whitney and get to the testing center when I couldn't even walk. It wasn't an easy undertaking, but I was determined to let nothing stand between that test and me. The pain was excruciating. I took some Tylenol, iced it, wrapped it tightly with an old ace bandage and pressed on toward my mission. The pain didn't let up at all. Fortunately, when I dropped Whitney off at her grandma's house and she saw the way I was walking, or rather hopping, she offered me an old pair of crutches. I was able to get into the testing site without looking too conspicuous. I honestly think I would have crawled in if that is what it took. Much to my surprise, I aced my placement exam even testing out of several classes. Maybe I wasn't as dumb as I had been led to believe. The next step was to decide what I wanted to go to school for. This time it was absolutely my decision and I didn't have a clue. My mind was a little more practical at this stage in my life and I was leaning toward something with job security. I was given a test to see where my interests and strengths were to get a good fit for my personality, but in my mind, I knew I wanted something that paid well and that would be in high demand. My mind went toward the medical field and I briefly considered nursing. This was the time when AIDS was first coming into the public light. Little was known about it and fear was rampant, including in my mind. I thought it wouldn't be wise to be working with blood, when chances were, I would be caring for many of these unfortunate victims who had contracted this vicious disease. I finally settled on Physical Therapy. The advisor explained that there was an assistant's degree that only took two years to obtain, but I wasn't interested in that. I wanted to be the therapist. I wanted the respect that came with being in charge and, besides, I reasoned, I was in no hurry. Nothing was going to happen to my husband for many years so I could spend a bit longer getting my degree. The advisor was less than enthusiastic about my choice. She told me that unless I had dreamed all my life about becoming a physical therapist, I should rethink my major because it was virtually impossible to achieve this lofty goal. She explained that the PT program was very difficult to get into and unless I made all A's I could forget about even applying. I silently wondered why people were always telling me that I couldn't do what I wanted to do. I had let my parents, principal, guidance counselor and husband dissuade me years ago and was not about to let this stranger do the same. If I failed, then I failed, but I would not let her tell me I couldn't do it. I dug my heels in and doggedly signed up for my first semester of prerequisite classes. The list was daunting including anatomy and physiology, chemistry and physics, but I didn't let that hamper my excitement. I returned home that day feeling quite pleased with all that had been accomplished. For the first time in years, I felt like I was regaining control of my life that had been vicariously spinning out of control. By the time I returned home, my ankle had swollen to three times its normal size and was throbbing with pain. It had turned a deep purple color around my ankle-bones and down the bottom side of my foot, making it obvious to me that it was broken. Having no insurance and no money for a doctor I just had to doctor myself. I pumped the Tylenol, kept it wrapped, iced it and tried to stay off it as much as possible. Nothing seemed to ease the pain and no matter what position I placed it in, it hurt just the same. Even the pain of a broken bone paled in comparison to the excitement that was welling up inside of me. As my ankle slowly healed, so began the healing of my spirit that had been broken so many years ago. I had begun to slowly, and ever so slightly, believe in myself again.

As I began my classes, I was again hit with the stark reality of the evils of this world. I had a Humanities class in which the professor made it clear on the first day of class that he didn't believe in God. He even went as far as to refer to the Bible as a storybook full of myths. I sat in my seat dumbstruck. I had never heard such talk. How could someone say these things? I sadly looked around at my predominantly much younger classmates and was struck with the notion that many of these people may believe the nonsense that this learned professor was spewing. As my ears and face began burning, I could sit quietly no more and, to my surprise, found myself speaking out loud in disagreement with the lies he was spouting. He taunted that even the Bible says there are many other gods and that the children of Israel worshiped many other gods. I calmly explained to him that the Bible does not say there are many gods and that the children of Israel were worshiping idols and false gods. The conversation went on for 10 to 15 minutes back and forth, no doubt with God giving me the words to come back with each argument this man produced. When he finally determined that I was not going to back down he stated that it was obvious that I had a predetermined mindset and that nothing he could say was going to change that. I told him that I had an open mind and that if he could prove to me otherwise, I would believe what he said. He ended the conversation with a snide remark about it being Monday and that he wasn't prepared to prove anything on a Monday. I sat quietly in my seat fuming and fearing that this may be a very long semester. After a few minutes of lecturing, he looked up at the ceiling and quipped, "Well God hasn't struck me dead, so I must be telling the truth." Indeed, it was going to be a very long semester. A couple of days later, as I was walking back to his classroom, I was filled with dread. Would he begin propagating his lies again today? I glanced nervously toward his classroom door and to my dismay, saw him walking steadfastly toward me. I caught my breath and walked just as determinedly toward him. I would not be bullied by this professor. I steeled myself for round two but to my surprise he didn't want to fight. Instead, he began taking back all his assertions from the class before, claiming he was afraid I had misunderstood what he was trying to say. I knew in my heart I had not misunderstood anything, rather he had decided that it would be too much work to lead this class astray with someone in it that would not just sit idly by and let him do it. I politely stated that I was glad to hear that he was not as misguided as I had feared and walked satisfied into the classroom pondering what had just happened. Had I just stood up to this intellectual and won? How did that just happen? I knew in my heart that it was only through God giving me the words to speak. However; my confidence grew exponentially from this experience. Maybe there was hope for me yet. Maybe, I would not be destined to be a failure in life. The professor never broached the subject of God the rest of the semester, and of all the knowledge I gleaned from his class, this first lesson would be the most valuable.

While things were going well at school, things at home took a turn for the worse. One evening after dinner, Brandon asked me to go for a walk with him. This was very odd as he usually just wanted to sit staring mindlessly at the television when he was home, but the thought of a little one on one with my husband excited me. I chatted about the day's events, but he seemed distracted. This wasn't entirely new as I often felt he could care less about what the kids and I were up to. Then he dropped the bomb. He told me that he was cheating on me and that he had been ever since Chad was a baby. I nervously laughed and told him that he wasn't funny. As we stopped and faced each other on that desolate back road I could see in his eyes that he wasn't joking. I struggled to process what he was saying. This seemed sur-real. I numbly walked back toward our house trying to make this make sense. It was all so confusing. I was blindsided by this news. When I asked him what he wanted, he coldly stated that he wanted out. This hit me like a brick to the face. Really? He wanted out? He wanted a divorce from me? The wife who had given everything for 12 years of her life to try to make him happy while placing her needs on the back burner was now being dumped? Not only that but I had foolishly chosen to believe that he loved me, and he had been playing me for at least nine of those years. I really was a fool. How could I have missed this? What world had I been living in? As we returned home the weight of his words finally sank in and I began to cry. I looked to the man I had married. The man who was supposed to care for me, love me and make everything better but was met with calloused laughter. Who was this man? He was a far cry from that charming teenager I had fallen for 13 years earlier.

With the weight of hiding his affairs off his shoulders, he became much more brazen with his extra-curricular activities. I found movie tickets in his pants pock-ets, which hurt way worse than you would think. He never took me to the movies. We never had the money. He would now come home from work, shower, shave put on aftershave and prepare for his dates with other women. He now had nothing to hide and therefore was doing nothing to hide it. In desperation, after begging him to stay home with me one night I asked him what exactly it was that he wanted. After about three seconds of silence he replied, "I want to have my cake and eat it too." How had I ended up here? I was lost. I had no clue what to do. The next day as I struggled to sort things out, I decided to go and speak with the minister of the church the kids and I had been attending. I told him of my husband's recent revela-tion and asked him what I should do. For some reason, I left out the part about the abuse. In fact, it never even crossed my mind that he was abusive. The only thing in my mind was that I was on the verge of losing my marriage, which meant the kids lost their dad. The preacher asked me a pointed question that day. He asked me what I wanted. I couldn't even form a complete thought at this point let alone know what I wanted. He explained that due to my husband's infidelity, I was totally justified to file for divorce. It was now just a matter of deciding if I wanted to be done with this or if I wanted to attempt to repair this damaged marriage. I prayed about it and turned my options over in my head. I didn't want a divorce. Divorce equals failure and, besides, how could I take the kids away from their father? That would be such a selfish thing to do. I convinced myself that he was a good dad and loved his kids and I didn't want them to come from a divorced family. I married for better or for worse and I was determined to stick to those vows. I just had to figure out how to make him want to work it out. He had made it plain and clear that he didn't want to work on this. He was ready to move on. As I mulled the situation over in my head, I knew what I had to do. I had to change his mind. I had to make him want to make this work. I had already tried being the dutiful, faithful wife and that certainly didn't draw him to me, so I would pretend to be moving on myself. With all his insanely jealous actions of the past, I concluded that this would be my best move. I went to the beauty shop and got a much-needed perm, began tanning and made sure to always look top notch. I also began loading the kids in the car and dropping them off at the shop, when his workday was finishing up. I could tell this piqued his interest, as he quizzically inquired as to where I was going. I flippantly responded, "don't worry about it. You don't want me." Dumbfounded, he then asked what time I would be home. I coyly replied that I wasn't sure and left before he could attempt to stop me. Wow did that feel good! As I drove away, I felt as though I had taken a little of the power back in this relationship. I was no longer just a passenger on this horrific ride he had taken me on. For once I was in the driver's seat. Now if I could just figure out what to do. It was 7:00 pm and this strait-laced mother of three was headed out on the town. You can only do so much window-shopping and most of the stores closed by 9:00. I had no girl friends to hang out with and I had never stepped foot in a bar or club. There's not a whole lot for a person like that to do after 9:00 on a Friday night so I went to Wal-Mart. They were open 24 hours and I was determined to make this night out last long enough to be believable. I pushed the empty cart around the store for five hours while pondering my plight. I hoped this would work and I could somehow save my marriage.

It only took a few faux dates for my plan to work its magic. He now had a renewed interest in the wife he was ready to discard a few weeks earlier. He suddenly was around more, and much more attentive. This seemed so easy. It was quite satisfying that I had been able to manipulate the situation by making him realize what he was about to lose. Then one day, approximately six months later, I began to get an uneasy feeling. While he slept, I snatched his wallet and took it into the living room. I quickly rummaged through it looking for any kind of evidence that he was still up to his old tricks and I promptly found what I was looking for. It was a folded-up paper with the name Carla on it and a phone number scrawled beneath it. I called the number and asked the woman on the other end of the line why her number was in my husband's wallet to which she replied, "If you were keeping him happy at home, he wouldn't be looking for it somewhere else." So that was that. I guess that left little doubt as to what he was doing. I realized that he had most likely never stopped. I had believed what I wanted to believe, and he only went back into hiding his indiscretions rather than flaunting them. After that phone call, I felt a shift deep down inside of me. I would not let him continue to hurt me. My heart became as cold as ice. When he dressed up and went out, I felt nothing. When he stayed home with his family, I felt nothing. I truly had no feelings one-way or the other. I resolved in my heart to stay married to this pitiless man for the children. Just because I wasn't happy with their father, didn't mean they deserved to grow up without him. Somehow the abuse we were living in had been buried deep within my subconscious and was not factored into my decision to stay. I began simply going through the motions in my marriage. I cooked, cleaned and did everything I had done for years, minus my heart. He would never get that again. I began walking daily to try to preserve a tiny bit of my sanity. Walking was my therapy. I would repeat, "You are worthwhile! He is an idiot!" over and over in my head as I doggedly stormed along the back roads near my house.

Brandon felt the shift in my heart too, and his response was to be more aggressive. The abuse of the kids escalated, and he became more verbally abusive and threatening to me. Many nights he ranted and raved deep into the night while carrying one of his many guns around. He was convinced that my lack of love toward him meant I had someone else. In his mind, the only reason that I would have lost my love and devotion toward him, was if I were having an affair. He would menacingly pace about, pointing the gun in my face and shouting that the only way he could ever live without me is if I were dead. Other times he would say that he couldn't live without me and was going to shoot himself. On many occasions, he retreated behind the house with his gun and I would wait optimistically by the window listening for the gunshot, willing him to just do it and end this nightmare already. But time after time he returned to the house too cowardly to even finish out his constant threat.

During this time, we made one of our few trips to Indiana for a visit. We were staying upstairs at my parent's house in the room that had been my refuge as a child.

During the night, I awoke and immediately sensed that something was wrong. Brandon was covered in sweat. I tried to arouse him, but he was unable to move or even speak. I knew this condition. He was having a low blood sugar, but this time it was lower than I had ever seen before. Usually, he would just go eat a candy bar or drink a pop, but he wasn't going anywhere this time. As I stared at this man who had brought me so much pain, I realized that his life was in my hands. I could roll over and go back to sleep and he would be dead by morning. This was the perfect escape. I would not be subjected to his constant abuse, nor would the children, and I would not be judged by my friends and family for getting a divorce. I would be the poor widow who lost her husband way too soon. No one would ever know. No one but me and God that is. My heart sank as I realized that I could not do this. I quickly crept downstairs to the kitchen where I found some orange juice and returned to his side. I had learned that orange juice was the best solution to quickly raise blood sugar. He was so far gone that he couldn't swallow but orange juice has the special property of being able to be absorbed through the membranes in your mouth and under your tongue. After several doses of the juice, he aroused enough for me to be able to help him down the stairs and into our car where I quickly drove him to the ER. He was still unable to speak, and his muscles were not working correctly. The emergency doctor told us that he had suffered a mini-stroke during the incredibly low blood sugar and was lucky to be alive. I didn't feel so lucky. I wished he were dead, but I knew his life was not mine to take.

One would think that if a person saved your life, you would have an attitude of gratitude, but Brandon didn't. Upon returning home, nothing changed. He was still the mean cruel man who ruled our house. As I surveyed the situation, I realized that he was harsh to our first-born, but Monty was tough and didn't cry so this appeased his wrath. Chad was more soft-hearted and would scream out in horror for me to save him, which served to intensify his father's anger, and he got it twice as bad. Then there was Whitney. She never suffered one blow from her father's hands or feet, but she suffered mentally. She was constantly demeaned and told she was worthless and could do nothing right. Then there was me. I was just frantically trying to keep it together. Trying to run interference and avoid the next blow up. In my limited knowledge, I thought Chad was the one who was being messed up the most, but in each of us he was changing us down to the core.

Chad age 8, Monty age 10, and Whitney age 6

That final Sunday night, as we were preparing for dinner, Monty did it. He screwed up by wearing a necklace through the living room. It wasn't girly or anything. It was a necklace that a young man would wear but it enraged his father. Brandon flew into a rage saying that no son of his was going to dress like that. He began wailing on Monty getting him down in the hallway, punching him wildly and kicking him with his boots. He was out of his mind and was not listening as I pleaded with him to stop. My mere 118 pounds was no match for his substantial frame that had once attracted me to him, and he threw me off like a bug. When the barrage finally ended, I ran to Monty to make sure he was ok. He stared into my eyes and through tears he boldly whispered, "If he ever touches me again, I will kill him." This hit me like a ton of bricks. How had we gotten here? When did my dream for happily ever after turn into this nightmare? I assured Monty that I would take care of it and told him that it was not his job to do that. I implored him to give me a little while and I would get him out of this unbearable situation. Later that night I called my brother and guardedly asked him what constitutes abuse. This was the first I had spoken of my little family's dark secret. He was stunned by what I divulged and told me to just say the word and he would be in Florida to pick us up. I told him to give me a little time to work the details out and put him on standby. This was a tricky situation that would require some clever planning. I didn't know what Brandon's reaction would be if he thought he was about to lose his family. We were his possessions and, I feared, that when faced with losing us he would kill us all and then kill himself. He had threatened it often enough. Then there was the added complication of finals. I was to begin my finals the next day, and if I didn't complete them, an entire semester of school would be lost, and I needed my education now more than ever. Brandon's outbursts typically would occur once every couple of weeks and I thought I could easily complete my college finals within the week and then we would make our escape the following week. We would just have to all be very careful to not do anything to set him off.

The following day the kids went off to school and I went off to college to complete day one of finals and everything went as planned for me until I returned to my van in the college parking lot. There was a note on my windshield from my sister-in-law Debbie. It said the boy's school wanted me to call them. I drove the few blocks to her house and called and was directed to a police officer that told me, "We have your children and we are not letting them back into your home. What are you going to do about it?" I told him I would be right there and hung up the phone with my heart racing. I immediately flew to the school and was escorted into a room with several police officers and school administrators. The story, that unfolded, was somehow surprising to me. Apparently, word had traveled around school that the boys' dad owned many guns and that these guns were missing. The boys were called into the principal's office to get to the bottom of things. It was the principal's fear that these guns had somehow ended up at school. He worried that they had been stolen by someone who would come in and shoot up the school or that the boys had brought them to school. The boys were placed in separate rooms and interrogated by police officers. After several hours, Chad broke down and admitted that he had taken them and hid them behind the couch because he was afraid his daddy was going to kill his mommy. Yep, that was our life, but it sounded so bad when someone said it out loud. I blankly told the police officer that we were done. I was planning to leave as soon as finals were over, but we would leave immediately and never go back. They needed more than my word and asked me to call someone to come and get us. As I dialed my mother's phone number, I was filled with dread but at this point I had no choice. Upon hearing my voice, she immediately knew something was wrong and I began pouring out the details of our secret life right there on the phone. I told her everything that came to mind and realized that I was seeing my life as it truly was for the very first time. I began remembering the abuse of the animals and the threats to my life and most horrifically the constant abuse of the children. I do not remember her response, but the plan was hatched for my father and brother to set out on a road trip to pick us up. The police offered a women's shelter for Whitney and I to stay in but explained that the boys would have to stay in a separate shelter due to regulations. I told them that was not an acceptable situation and that I felt they needed their mother now more than ever. They agreed to let us go to Debbie's house, since she had recently filed for divorce from Brandon's brother and would keep our location a secret if asked. So, we went into hiding there. An armed guard was provided that next day so that I could finish my finals. I have no clue how I was able to think of anything other than the crazy hurricane that had become my life, but somehow, I passed every single one. My dad and brother arrived, and we went to stay with them in a hotel that last night in Florida. Debbie had heard that Brandon was not staying at the house and that he had gone to his mother's, so before heading back to Indiana, we stopped, apprehensively, for a quick grab and go. I instructed the kids to go into their rooms and grab the things that were the most important to them. I was so afraid he would return home before we got out of there and kill us all, but God was watching out for us. The kids each got as much as their little arms could carry and as I went back to check on Whitney she innocently asked if she had to leave too because her daddy didn't hit her. Terror shot through my entire body at the thought of leaving her with this man. I explained to her that even though he didn't hit her, that Mommy could never live without her little girl. This explanation seemed to appease her worries and she loaded her prized possessions into the getaway vehicle. The boys followed suit and I too grabbed a few items including the family dog and we headed off into the night never looking back. We drove away in silence leaving this nightmare behind, or so I thought. I rode along in a daze. I couldn't feel relieved or happy or even sad. I felt nothing but empty and cold, as we traveled back to my childhood home to begin life over again.

8
NEW DREAMS

Moving back home with mom and dad with three active children was not ideal, but we did what we had to do, and my parents graciously conceded. I immediately began looking for a job. I feared that it would not be easy because of the way Brandon had always struggled to make money. I was even less prepared for the job market than he. He, at least, had a trade and some work experience. Me, I had nothing. I was quickly hired by Cracker Barrel and got a quick lesson in tipping etiquette. I had no clue that servers only made $2.13 per hour and their tips were what they lived on. Not that I had any experience with tipping anyway, we never went out to eat anywhere other than McDonald's. Still it came as quite a surprise when I found out how little I would be making. Despite the pay, I found working at Cracker Barrel a joy and I wore my khakis, white oxford shirt and brown apron proudly. It had been easy to land my first job. Each server had his or her own section of the restaurant and I quickly ascertained that the pocket change and lint that was left by most of our senior citizen patrons was not going to add up too much. On the rare occasion that someone got a five-dollar bill we were all celebrating. This job would do for now. It was better than nothing, but I immediately went back to the job search and was quickly hired to work at Pizza Hut. Working here was a step up because they paid minimum wage, $5.15 per hour, but it still wasn't much after taxes. Pizza Hut was tough during the lunch shift. They had a buffet and each server was responsible for about half of the restaurant. Things got hectic quickly and no one tips well when they go to a buffet. I tried my best to keep up, but I was new to this waitress thing and it got confusing as to which tables were mine and who ordered what. One time I almost got a beat down for taking my coworkers two-dollar tip off one of her tables. I quickly gave it back to her when confronted, but I don't think she believed me when I told her it was an accident. Flustered, I tried harder to keep track of what I was doing but after dumping a tray of eight drinks onto a customer's lap, I wondered if I would ever be able to get the hang of this. After only two weeks on the job, I shamefully turned in my resignation. It was not like me to quit on something, but I had three children to support and needed money, plus, I had landed the big one. I had been hired at the Richmond Red Lobster, and after only a few days on the job it was apparent that this place was a gold mine. Why waste my time on pocket change when I could make $10 an hour in tips on average at Red Lobster? I gladly said goodbye to Cracker Barrel and Pizza Hut, as the Red Lobster gang became my second family. I worried that they only allowed you to work 3 tables at a time, but it seemed to work out ok for the most part. The trays were huge, fortunately I never dropped one. There seemed to be two types of people working the restaurant scene, lifers and college students. The lifers were older and had worn faces with no hope on them and the college students worked with a little more lilt in their steps as they knew this was only a temporary situation. I took my place amongst them and set my mind to be the best server I could be. There was one girl who made more than the rest of us. She consistently had the most money when the night ended. I tried to watch her to see how she did it and she downright rocked it. She turned those tables faster than anyone else and although her tips were not truly larger, she got people in and out faster. Maybe one day I would be that fast, but for the time being I had to bank on being friendly and efficient and trying to make each guest's dining experience pleasant in hopes that it would pay off in the end.

Since I was now able to work and make a living, I determined that I needed to buy my own car. Along with money I was able to set back from waitressing and a little left over from my school money, I had $1200. I quickly found out that I couldn't get much for that amount. My husband, who was trying gallantly to win me back, offered to buy me a car through the auto auction. Out of desperation, I agreed, and he brought me a pretty little 1989 red Eclipse. My joy was short lived however, when it quit on me only a month later. I spent the rest of my savings and he got me another Eclipse but this one was black. It was kind of fun running around in a cute little sports car and it suited me just fine for driving the 23 miles back and forth to Richmond where I was working and going to school.

The longer I worked at Red Lobster, the better I got at it. I learned to try to connect with each guest in some way. This was not in my nature. I was painfully shy and backward and really would prefer that no one look at me, but if I wanted to make money, not only did I need them to look at me, I needed them to like me. Lunch shifts were notorious for bad tipping. The total bill was always low and therefore the tips would be low as well. A couple of dollars was par for the course and by the end of the shift you may have only made $20. One Saturday afternoon by chance, I received the most tattered, torn and dirty old five-dollar bill as a tip. The bill was so nasty that I didn't want to even touch it, but then I had an idea. If my first impulse was that I didn't want to pick up that five and put it into my pocket, would others feel the same way? Was it possible that by giving that five back to my guests all day long on my low paying lunch shift, I could get it back as a tip? The experiment was on. All morning and afternoon, I gave my guests their change, making sure that they got that special five-dollar bill along with the crispest, cleanest and newest one-dollar bills I could find, and it worked like a charm. That "filthy five" came back time after time and I found myself receiving $5 tips for each meal rather than $2 tips. This was quite the revelation and would become a tactic I used for the remainder of my serving career. Serving was hard work. Due to my college schedule, my availability was limited and in order to make enough money to support three children I worked double shifts every Friday, Saturday and Sunday. Red Lobster was great to work with me on this, but a double shift standing on your feet and running back and forth to keep your guests happy was exhausting. By the end of the night my feet hurt so badly I could barely walk, but I pressed on. I had something to accomplish. My attempts to connect with my guests seemed to work for the most part and I began to have regulars, who asked for me. Not all were great tippers, but a request often meant you would be able to pick up a fourth table, so that raised your overall tips. One of my regulars was a loud but friendly couple who ran me to death. Every stop by their table ended with a trip to the kitchen for 4 more items. The wife always ordered two Ranch and two French dressings for her salad and turned it into soup. She then ordered the most fattening item on the menu, the Admiral's Feast, which was all of the seafood items, deep fried in oil and a baked potato with extra butter and sour cream and then she topped it off with a diet coke. Another table, which became a request table started out as a charity pick up. This couple came in every Sunday after church and no one wanted to serve them. She was an angry old biddy who strode into the restaurant ahead of her stroke affirmed husband growling at him to hurry up. He was quiet and unassuming, and I was instantly drawn to him. It was the runt of the litter syndrome that my mother had diagnosed me with early on in life I am sure, but I felt so sorry for this elderly man. How sad to spend your life with someone so grumpy and cruel. She never let him speak and would order for the both of them, ordering the lunch chicken finger meal, with fries and an extra plate for him on which she would dole out his meager portion. She would then drink a coke and order him water. As if watching this poor treatment of an impaired senior citizen was not bad enough, your final payment for your service was always the same, $1. No one wanted to wait on this couple, and everyone ran the other way when they entered the restaurant. I finally told the seater that every time this couple entered the restaurant, I wanted them seated in my section. The first Sunday following the birth of my new quest, I wrote down their order on a piece of paper and then stuck it in the back of my book. I would make them feel special. This table was not about the tip, I knew what my tip would be. This became about making the crotchety old lady happy, in hopes that she would then be just a bit nicer to the poor old man. My goal was to make her smile. The next Sunday, I watched the door for their entrance and was at their table with their drinks as soon as they sat down, greeting them warmly and inquiring if they wanted the usual. The old lady looked up at me in shock and stammered that yes, they would and as I turned to leave, I made eye contact with her husband and he grinned at me. I winked at him and knew he was on to my scheme. Their food arrived quickly, and I felt that ice-cold exterior melting just a little, but really saw no change in her behavior. Week after week, I persevered until she finally started loosening up a bit. Everybody wants to feel special and that they are worth remembering. To my amazement, I found myself looking forward to their arrival. She began smiling more and talking a little softer. My goal had been accomplished. I had won her over with a little special treatment. This was even further proven that monumental Sunday, when she reached into her wallet and pulled out not one but two, one-dollar bills for me. Even though this amount of money is small, the fact that it came from her made this the biggest tip I ever received. This couple had become one of my favorite regulars.

I had another man who became a regular. I found myself watching for him to arrive and he was there weekly asking for me. He always ordered the same thing, soup and salad with a mega margarita for lunch, and then he would leave me a twenty-dollar tip, which was more than his meal cost. I looked forward to his visit not only for the guaranteed twenty bucks but also for the conversation. He seemed to really care about me and my life. He had told me about his wife and small son and the business he had built from the ground up. He was quite an impressive man. I enjoyed our conversations. It was nice to have a friend who wanted nothing in return. When March rolled around and he happened to be in on my birthday, he left me a $100 tip. I should have known something was up. No one gives someone $100 without expecting something in return. Shortly after that, he offered to take me shopping. He said he wanted me to have some nice clothes. I was excited at the thought of having some nice things to wear. Money was tight and everything I made seemed to go to the kids, but something just felt wrong about it. I politely declined his offer, but he kept coming back. The day finally arrived when his true motives came out. He asked me to go out on a date with him. I was taken aback. This wasn't like that. We were friends. He was married. What about his son? My mind was scrambling as I tried to make sense of this. When I could speak again, I simply asked him one question, "What would your wife think of that?" I no longer liked this man. He reminded me of my husband, so quickly willing to throw his family away for a good time. I never saw this man again. I guess the game was over.

There were lots of other games to be played, however, and I learned to play them well. One particularly slow afternoon a table of three businessmen sat down in my section. As usual, I strained to hear their conversation to find something to connect with them on. I laughed and joked with them, offering my advice on their business, which was met with jovial laughter. One of the men then asked, "Isn't that man sitting across from me the ugliest man you have ever seen?" I was appalled. He was not particularly handsome, but I would not have called him ugly. I strongly disagreed with him, but as I left the table a plan was hatched. I asked all my female coworkers to slowly stroll by the table and pause to look this guy up and down in a deliberately obvious way and then walk away without saying anything. It didn't take the men long to catch on to what was going on and the table would erupt with laughter every time the next server would stop by. Just before giving them their bill I quickly wrote out a mock survey on a piece of paper with the categories handsome, homely and doesn't hurt to look at him and then put tally marks by the categories with handsome winning by a landslide. I delivered the results along with the bill and was rewarded with robust laughter from the three gentlemen. The man who had initially asked the question and who was obviously in charge then asked how much of a tip he owed me. I coyly asked what an evening of entertainment was worth to them and walked away. When they were gone, I discovered they left behind a $130 tip, which was more than their total bill. I guess it was safe to say they enjoyed their business meeting.

I learned that being overly friendly with the men only worked when their wives were not around. One kind elderly man was overtly enjoying the banter and got more and more friendly with each drink. Finally, after he attempted to order another his wife snapped at him that she thought he had had quite enough. While she sat glaring at me, I feared that my tip had just gone down the drain. But then I saw my opportunity; she got up and went into the bathroom. I quickly delivered the bill in hopes that I could salvage this tip with her out of the way and it worked. He tipped me very well and she was none the wiser. I was learning what my parents meant when they cautioned that alcohol would make you do things you might not otherwise do. My tips were often notably higher when someone had a bit too much to drink.

This fact became even more clear to me one evening when I had a table of four couples who were enjoying the liquor and really making me work for my tip. The women ran me all night and by chance as the night was ending, one man laid down a tip and another absentmindedly started to pick it up. I called him out in front of the group and asked if he were getting ready to snatch my tip, which resulted in gales of laughter from the group. He then proceeded to prove that he didn't want my money, by reaching into his wallet and throwing some bills down on the table. The other men responded by doing the same and it quickly became a contest to see who could lay a bill down last. I smiled as I realized what was happening and they were all too drunk to notice. They left me an obscene tip, but it was nights like those that were helping me to take care of my babies.

Everything was not fun and games at work. Some customers were mean and cranky and treated me so badly that I wanted to cry. There was only one who succeeded, and he was relentless. I typically would just give it right back to these grumpy old men and they would eventually be won over by my charm, as evidenced by one man who started out the evening determined to make mine miserable but ended the night by offering to introduce me to his son stating that I would make a wonderful addition to his family. I am not sure if I was just worn down or if this one man was as cold as steel, but he won. Maybe it was just a moment of weakness that day, but when I asked what I could get him and he said another server, that was the straw that broke the camel's back. I gladly obliged but the rejection sent me into a flurry of tears. The manager later informed me that he felt he had waited too long for his drink, not understanding that it had to be made by the busy bartender. Overall, I would say the good outweighed the bad and Red Lobster ended up being the most perfect means to my desired end. They would work around my school schedule and I could consistently make $100 per day to take care of my family. The fact that I, having absolutely no work experience, was able to instantaneously make more than my husband was not lost on me. Day by day, I would begin to see things more clearly.

Although greatly appreciated, living back at home with my mother was not the best situation. I suppose it could have been predicted that we would naturally fall back into the roles we last held when living together, but everything seemed to be exponentially worse. Even though I had been living on my own, raising 3 children and running a household, I felt as though my mother thought I was clueless about how to live successfully. She proceeded to mother me, asking me if I turned off the lights, made my bed, brushed my teeth along with feeling compelled to tell me how I should and should not dress. I quickly knew that this living arrangement was not going to work out as a long-term solution. My mother and father owned a trailer that was situated on a lot adjoining their property and they agreed to rent it to me. This seemed to be an ideal solution. The kids and I could have a bit of privacy, but Mom and Dad would be close enough to help when I needed to work.

As I settled into this new life of working as a waitress, being a single mom of 3 and finishing up my pre-requisite courses at IU East, I discovered that nothing worth having ever comes easy. Some of my hard-earned credits from Florida didn't transfer and I found that by moving I had added an extra semester to my education. Although this felt like a kick in the gut, I pressed on. Besides, this allowed me the opportunity to take my first college art class and I chose pottery. I absolutely loved the feel of the wet clay in my hands as the pottery wheel spun below me. Apparently, my passion for art was attractive to the teacher. He was an older, artsy looking man who thought it was somehow appropriate to replay that pottery scene from Ghost with his student. As he pressed up against my backside, I wondered how he thought this was ok. I gracefully escaped this awkward situation and made a mental note to keep myself at arm's length from this beatnik. I somehow was able to complete the class with only a few more instances of attempted molestation and emerged with an A in the class. This would not be the last obstacle I had to overcome while completing my college education.

One of my psychology classes became very difficult to endure. One day, when the topic was child abuse, I broke down while listening to an audio recording of an abusive altercation between a father and his child. As I sat in my seat listening, I was transported back in my mind to our days in Florida. Chad had once again angered his father and was curled up in a ball on the floor pleading with me to rescue him. I could see his tiny little hands reaching to me, hear his sad little voice pleading "Mommy, mommy help me," along with his terrified face and questioning eyes asking, "Why aren't you saving me?" That is the question I struggle with to this day. Why did I stay for so long? What kind of mother would allow her children to be beaten? What have I done to them? If a child can't count on his mother, who can he trust? I began sobbing uncontrollably and had to get up and leave the classroom. It was obvious to me, if to no one else that I had a lot to work through. Eventually, this class would provide me with a means to begin working through some of this. We were given an assignment called a "feeling letter." The assignment was to choose someone who had hurt us in life and follow the prescribed format writing a letter to them and then writing the response that we needed to hear back from them. This was my letter.

Dear Brandon,

I am angry that you let me down. I am angry that you hurt the kids and made me be a bad mother by letting you. I am angry that you cheated on me. I am angry that you didn't love me enough not to. I am angry that I now have to do it all. I am angry that I can't be home with the kids because I have to work. I am angry that you won't send me money to help out.

I am sad that we aren't forever. I am sad that our perfect love fell apart. I am sad that the kids don't have the perfect family anymore. I am sad that I don't have you. I am sad that I am alone. I am sad that all of our dreams will never be anything more than old dreams.

I am afraid that I will be alone forever. I am afraid that people will judge me and think I am bad. I am afraid that the kids will be or have already been permanently damaged by this, by you. I am afraid that the boys will hurt our grandbabies, they seem so angry. I am afraid I will never be happy again.

I am sorry that I wasn't the wife you needed me to be. I am sorry that I wasn't good enough. I am sorry I left you all alone and now you are sick all alone. I am sorry that you can't see your kids. I am sorry that the fairytale has ended. I am sorry that I don't want to be with you anymore. I am sorry that I wasn't good enough.

I want to be happy. I want for you to be happy without me. I want someone to love me. I need someone to love me. I want to feel safe. I want to be taken care of. I want to be carefree. I want the kids to be happy. I want to feel good about myself again. I want to be a good mother. I need help. I can't do this all by myself forever. I feel as though I am about to break.

I forgive you for not being who I needed you to be. I forgive you for... no I don't forgive you. I understand that you have reasons for being who you are, but you hurt us, and I don't think this hurt will ever go away. I know that you love us, but in a way that I don't understand. I know that you want us back, but I am too scared.

Thank you for listening to me. Thank you for not hurting me. Thank you for talking to me rationally. Thank you for giving me three beautiful babies.

This is the letter I wrote as if from him, telling me the things I needed to hear.

Response

Dear Stacy,

Thank you for telling me your feelings. I am sorry that I destroyed your love for me. I am sorry for betraying your love and for breaking the promises that I made to you on our wedding day. I am sorry that I put you in the middle between me and the kids. I am sorry that I made you be a bad mother.

I understand that I have broken something that can't be fixed. I understand that you have to protect the kids as well as yourself from me.

You deserve better than me. You deserve someone who will love you, respect you, and treat you like a princess. You are so smart, hard-working and such a good mother. I really respect you for taking control when I was out of control. You are special. You are one of a kind and whoever you choose to give your love to is a very lucky man.

Thank you for the love you have given me for the past sixteen years.

I promise to send you money. I promise to never hurt you or the kids again. I promise to be the man you need me to be even if it's not with you.

Although I would never send it, this letter marked the beginning of my understanding of how therapeutic writing can be. You can get everything out that you want to convey without being interrupted, corrected or judged. I would also never get my desired response from my ex. All I have ever gotten from him are denials of any wrongdoing making that ever-elusive forgiveness even harder to grasp ahold of.

As I worked diligently to complete all the requirements to allow me to apply to IUPUI's therapy program, I learned that I would have to complete observation hours in my desired field prior to applying. My first observation was in the outpatient physical therapy department at Reid hospital. The director was a tall burly man with the personality of a teddy bear. He allowed me to observe the wound debridement of a 25-year-old intellectually challenged girl. As we walked into the treatment room I was filled with nervous anticipation. I had no clue what I was about to witness but I had loved my advanced biology class. I fondly reminisced about my escapades while dissecting that 30-pound monstrosity of a cat. Rather than finding it repulsive and heartbreaking as I expected, I found it fascinating. I quickly learned all the required parts and, out of boredom, had become mischievous. We were supposed to be finding the feline's spleen, which I found in like three seconds. So, while the others were searching for theirs, I transplanted mine in my cat's mouth. I then requested help from my teacher, Mr. Shore, in finding the ever-elusive cat spleen. He dutifully sauntered over to assist and with a perplexed look on his face,

.earched and searched until I thought I would burst out laughing. Finally, I let him off the hook gleefully proclaiming, "Oh I found it! It is right here in his mouth." He slowly turned away, shaking his head as he walked away without a word. But that restrained smile I saw threatening to escape from his face told me that he was only pretending to be mad. I was abruptly snapped back to reality as the patient began whimpering fearfully while her bandages were being removed from her leg. I watched in fascination as their removal revealed a huge hole in her leg. The therapist began pulling out what I now know is packing material, but to me it looked like a giant never-ending tapeworm. As they pulled and pulled, the patient groaned and groaned and out of empathy for her pain, it was lights out for me. As it turns out, the big burly teddy bear is kind of nice to have around if you are going to pass out because he had noticed the blank stare in my eyes and had positioned himself to catch me before I slammed my head into the floor. It was all quite embarrassing and was making me question my career choice for the first time. As I watched a typical rehabilitation session, I found it disinteresting. Kick your leg like this 20 times. Ok, now the other one. It was not really that exciting, but I noticed across the gym there were more interesting things going on. One therapist was standing with her patient playing a game of cards and another was tossing a ball. I inquired as to what was going on over there and was told that it was called Occupational Therapy. That was my first exposure to this field, but I knew instinctively that this was so much more me. I would be able to use my creativity and make my treatments fun for my patients. So that is how I fell into my career. At that point I switched to Occupational Therapy and never looked back.

9

CHALLENGE ACCEPTED

As I looked into the OT program at IUPUI, I was told that I was not a viable candidate. It appeared that the OT program was in such high demand, that one of the requirements to be allowed to apply to the program was that your pre-requisites needed to have been completed predominantly at a college in Indiana. I had completed a year and a half in Florida before moving here and completing one year. That put me out of the running to even apply. So now what? Was this the end of my dream? No way! It couldn't be. I had three children depending on me, watching me to see how to react when life knocked them down. I would ask them to make an exception for me. Really? How stupid would one have to be to expect that the board of directors at IU in Bloomington would make an exception for a small-town girl who had irresponsibly gotten herself pregnant at 17 and now found herself a single mother of three living in a trailer, working as a waitress and trying to carve out a future for her family. Why would I be worthy of an exception? My father drove me on that long drive to Bloomington and I remember very little about the trip there, other than being terrified. That painfully shy part of me reared its ugly head again. I never wanted anyone to look at me. If I want a refill on my drink at the movie, too bad, I am not walking in front of all those people. If I need to use the bathroom after taking my seat in church, too bad, no way that is happening. I would rather be uncomfortable than be the center of attention. So now, I somehow had to muster the courage to convince big important people at IU, who had obviously made better choices in their lives, that I deserved a special exception. As I walked into that boardroom, my legs were trembling to the point that I thought they might fail to hold me up. I took my place, standing at the head of a mile-long table made of pristine mahogany wood and surrounded by a staunch army of business men in Armani suits looking at me with what I perceived as impatient irritation for stealing valuable time from their busy day. I took a deep breath and God took over. The words coming from my mouth were not my own, nor was the confidence I exuded. I told my tale of broken dreams of my childhood, my failed marriage and the one remaining dream that I was unwilling to relinquish for a future for my three babies. I pleaded with them to allow me the chance at that dream and as I finished there was not a dry eye in the place. They unanimously voted to allow me to apply to the OT program at IUPUI.

Although this was a giant step in the process it was nowhere near complete. I then had to apply to the program, along with 350 other hopefuls, and be selected to be one of 100 who would be allowed to interview for the meager 50 spots available in the program. I had been forewarned that many students apply three and four times before getting accepted and some end up walking away from their dream in defeat. In my mind, failure was not an option. I had to get in this year. My children were growing fast, as were the expenses that come along with raising three preteens. I needed to get my education completed so I could begin my career. Red Lobster was great as a temporary job, but honestly, it was not cutting it and I found myself taking out extra student loans to buy them clothes and shoes. To complicate matters, this would be the last year that the OT program could be completed with a bachelor's degree. After this class, anyone entering the program would have to complete a master's degree, which meant even longer to begin to make money. It was imperative that I be accepted into the program on my first attempt. I completed all the required paperwork and was granted an interview with the committee. It was all quite intimidating. Everything within me wanted to run, hide and give up but then I would look into my babies' eyes and know what I had to do. The interview was a bit more intimate than my first meeting at IU. This one was held in a small office with only three big wigs who comprised the school's OT committee responsible for choosing the best candidates for their program. Each committee member would ask one question which gave me three chances to impress them with my intelligence and to convince them that I was a better choice than at least half of the other hopefuls. During the interview they noticed that I was working full-time. They let me know that no one had ever successfully completed the OT program while working full-time. I don't believe it was meant to be a challenge, rather a warning, but I thought to myself, "challenge accepted." I also found the questions strange and not at all what I expected. One question I remember was about being a lifeguard at a pool and having multiple things happening all at once. I was then asked to put them in the order in which I would address them. My mind was swirling. What did this have to do with OT? Afterwards I realized the question was designed to test my logical reasoning skills and intelligence, which were skills required to successfully complete the program. I couldn't tell you how I answered but I must have done ok because about a month later, I received my acceptance letter in the mail!

When school began, I was introduced to two young OT hopefuls who were traveling from around the same area I was from. Our instructor recommended carpooling to help with the drive and expense. The girl's names were Angela and Brenda. Angela came from a very uppity family who did not allow their children to sit on the furniture. She told stories of being made to sit on the floor to watch TV and never being allowed to sit on their showcase pieces. She entered college, as was appropriate, right out of high school and was still living with her parents who were totally funding her college experience. We had nothing in common other than our goal to be an OT. Brenda on the other hand was a bit more like me. She had made some mistakes and had a toddler at home to show for it, but home was still at her parents. She had gotten pregnant in high school and never married her baby's daddy. Her parents were still funding her college to ensure a bright future for their child and grandchild. I envied her, not for the monetary support she was receiving, but for the emotional support.

My substandard car just could not hold up to the 140-mile round trip I had to drive to fulfill my part of the carpool agreement every third day, and after only a few short weeks it quit. The cost to repair was more than I had in it, so it seemed foolish to repair it. My maternal grandmother, who had been watching from afar, stepped up to the plate. She offered me her 1978 Chevy Impala. The kids fondly nicknamed it the "boat," but it quickly earned my appreciation for its reliability. It ran forever and got me through the rest of my college years. Brenda and Angela, however, were less than impressed with my new ride. They looked at it with disgust every time they got in it. After a couple of weeks, they came up with the idea that they should just take turns driving and I could pay for gas. That was ok with me, my car was eating me out of house and home being the gas hog it was. I would drive over each morning, meet them at a gas station along Interstate 70, hop in the back seat and we would be off. My responsibilities of working, parenting and studying began to weigh on me and I became more and more worn down. As Angela and Brenda chatted in the front seat, I often drifted off to sleep. I did not realize that this would become a source of frustration for them until the day they announced that I was kicked out of their carpool. They explained that it was unfair for only their cars to get the wear and tear on them and that I got to sit in the back seat and sleep while they were driving. These two selfish little girls dumbfounded me. They knew very well my situation and how difficult things were for me yet decided to self-centered-ly kick me to the curb with no sympathy for the load I was bearing. Now I would have to supply gas for the boat to drive that 140-mile round trip four days a week, as well as have to drive it alone with no one to help me stay awake. I was very hurt and angry with them, but the decision had been made. I quickly found a couple of new friends to hang with at school. They were no more like me than the first two as they were very young, but these two were genuine and kind and would remain my best buddies in the program throughout the remainder of time.

My life became a whirlwind. I went to Indianapolis Monday through Thursday, getting up at 5 am, applying makeup on the way, attending class all day and arriving back home again around 6 pm, before retreating to my bedroom to study until falling asleep in my books. Then Friday, Saturday and Sunday were filled with double shifts at Red Lobster. My children were neglected, and 8-year-old Whitney began filling the mother role for the family. She set her alarm to be sure she and her brothers got off to school on time, prepared dinner and did the laundry. I was torn. My emotions flip-flopped back and forth between wanting to be there for my children but needing to be an example of rising above your circumstances. My life had become nothing but work 100% of the time and something had to give. I needed some type of escape so I rationalized that going out with my friends from Red Lobster for a little while after getting off work may provide that outlet. It was nice to have a minute to just breathe and not think about anything. Day by day I pushed forward running on fumes.

Trying to deal with the aftereffects of abuse, support three kids on my own and complete a grueling OT program took everything I had to give and then some. My one-and-a-half-hour drive to and from school was treacherous not only because of driving while exhausted on the interstate but also because I was alone with my thoughts, my worries and my fears. Invariably my doubts would threaten to creep in and I would begin feeling beat down and worn out. On one particular day, just as I was needing a little extra incentive to keep going the sky turned what seemed to me, appropriately dark and the rains began to fall ever so lightly all around. I would have been content to continue to wallow in my misery however I noticed a rainbow directly ahead. My mind was transported back to childhood fantasies of finding the end of that rainbow and how nice it would be to find a pot of gold about now. As I drove, I wondered when the road would turn away from the rainbow because it looked as though I would drive right into it. I drove nearer and nearer until brilliantly and unexpectedly the end of the rainbow filled my entire car. I gloriously moved my arm through the prism of color and watched it change again and again. I thanked God for this much needed miracle as I was filled with a hope and a belief that anything was possible. God had just given me something even better than a pot of gold. He had given me hope. This would not be the last time God would remind me of His promise to take care of me.

I had never been into the party scene but 95% of the workers at Red Lobster were. I suppose that the serving industry kind of lends itself to that type of worker. You get immediate money on a nightly basis and don't have to get up early for work the next day. My friends would go to the clubs for drinking and dancing. I didn't have money to waste on drinks but that was never an issue as testosterone fueled guys who were under the influence and thought they might have a chance, kept the drinks coming. I had never drunk alcohol, so a little bit went a long way and after a couple of drinks I was really feeling it. I was then faced with the predicament of how to get back home safely while under the influence. One night when driving home I dozed momentarily and drifted slightly off the road. I was startled awake and spent the rest of the drive home evaluating what I was doing. What would happen if I got pulled over for drinking and driving or even worse wrecked and hurt myself or someone else? I presumed that could mean my children could be taken away and my hopes for a career could be ended. What was I thinking? It took only a couple nights of behaving badly for me to realize that I had too much to lose to be acting this way. I still felt the need for an escape though, so rather than stop going out I devised a plan to order a sprite with a dash of coke in it to give the appearance of drinking a hard drink. This worked well. Everyone but Kim, who was also a mother of three and understood me, thought I was one of them. My parents stood by and watched my behaviors and feared the worst. They never asked about drinking they just assumed, and I didn't offer up any reassurance. I was thoroughly annoyed at their constant intrusions into my adult life. In my mind, their assistance with the children and a cheap place to stay, did not give them the right to attempt to control my life. Once again, I reverted to a school child under the thumb of her over controlling parents. They would wait outside the door of my home for me to return in the wee hours of the morning and lecture me on how disappointed they were in me. I know they were worried that I may do something that would put me in danger, and I know they resented being responsible for my sleeping children while I went out with my friends from work. I only wished they could understand that I needed some outlet to keep from going insane. My life was one huge continuous stressor, between trying to raise three children, trying to complete my professional degree, and trying to make enough money as a waitress to support it all. Going out for an hour after work was my therapy, my release from stress. I had no intention of hooking up with or marrying some man I met in the bar and I had no intention of drinking or doing the many drugs, which were so prevalent in the server way of life. Even though I tried to fit in, everyone knew I didn't. They tolerated me to some extent but never fully trusted me due to my unwillingness to participate in the drug use. I found myself in the interesting predicament of not being accepted by my friends and coworkers because I didn't party hard enough and not being accepted by my parents because I partied too much.

At home, the relationship between my parents and I was strained. They were filled with worry and I was simply floating along feeling nothing. I didn't care that they were angry with me or disappointed in me. I didn't care that I barely had money to get through the week. I felt nothing. I remember the first time I realized that I had no feelings. My 8-year-old daughter had fallen and bloodied her knees and crawled up on my lap for comfort. I obligingly held her as she sobbed and as I looked down at her, wondered why I didn't care. I didn't necessarily want bad for her, but I also didn't hurt for her or feel saddened that she was hurt. What had happened to my empathy?

At some point during my marriage, I quit loving my husband. He was continually hurting me and my children, openly cheating on me and displayed little to no ambition of fixing our marriage. I think the respect went first and the love quickly followed. While I remained true to my marriage vows, I felt nothing. I merely went through the motions for the last couple of years. After leaving and getting my children to a safe place I began to process what had happened and I wondered what love really was. Was love just a theatrical production, something you make up in your mind? I remember at one point feeling as though I loved this man so much it brought tears to my eyes. Was I just play acting? What was wrong with me? Was this all pretend and not truly love? I struggled to figure it all out. How could love just leave? I thought love was something that when real, was forever. My love for my abusive husband was not forever. This challenged everything I believed about love. I knew my daddy's kind of love. He loved me no matter what. Why didn't my love stay no matter what? I have come to believe that my feelings for my husband began as an emotional excited response to someone I found attractive, definition number two in the Collins dictionary.

As I got to know him and spent time with him, I began to have a strong affection for him which grew even stronger when we were bound by marriage. I did love him, but one-sided love is unable to survive. As he proved over and over that he only loved himself, my love for him was choked out. I don't think it means it never was, but rather when it wasn't nurtured and fed it died. Lasting love is not a feeling of excitement. Love is a choice and after being hurt over and over I chose to let it go, almost as an instinctual protective response. The Bible says, "Let love be genuine. Abhor what is evil; hold fast to what is good." Is it any wonder the love I had for my abusive husband left me? I used to be such a caring person, but now nothing.

This coldness confused me, but I just continued to float along doing what I had to do with no emotional involvement. I think possibly shutting down my feelings was the only way I could leave my husband, take the kids away from their dad and do the hard things that needed to be done. Even if those emotions were tucked safely away from everyone around me, they had a way of slipping out in my dreams. At every mention of Brandon's name or any sight of a picture of him, all of those emotions would come that night when I laid down to sleep. I would have the most horrific nightmares. They were all the same. He was beating my children and I was unable to stop him. I would wake up in a panic, hyperventilating, sweating, crying, and looking about the room to ensure he wasn't there. That was always the end of my sleep for the night. I did not want to return to sleep for fear that the horror would return.

I was working to try to move on from the horror of my past and I knew I must be shrewd when it came to ending my relationship with my abusive husband, and I had a plan. I would be kind and civil until he tired of waiting around for my return and moved on to someone else. Occasionally he would call and say all the right things about how he was sorry and had changed intermingled with transferring the guilt to me saying, "Why didn't you just tell me you were going to leave if I didn't change?" I could not for the life of me figure out why one would need to be directly told that if he didn't stop beating the crap out of the kids, threatening his wife with a gun and spending his paycheck on other women, his wife might leave, but whatever. I was not fooled. However, I felt the only way to escape this alive was if he were the one to make the choice to divorce and move on.

Then one day as Christmas drew near, he asked to come stay with me for the holidays. He manipulatively maintained that he had no money for lodging and that the only way he could be with his children over the holidays is if I agreed to this. I caved. I told him he could come and stay in the trailer with us; however, he must understand that he would be sleeping on the couch in the living room and was only there as a guest. He acknowledged understanding but did not mean it. I would later learn that he viewed this as an attempt to reconcile. When he arrived, it was a bit uncomfortable for me, but the children were thrilled to have him around. I came to realize that no matter how poorly your dad treats you, he is still your dad and something deep inside of you longs for his acceptance. As the week went along, I went about my life as usual. School was on break, so I only had my work at Red Lobster. As I was leaving work one day, I glanced into my rearview mirror and saw what terrified me down to my core. It was him. He had come to Richmond to follow me to see if I was really working or if I was doing something else. I calmly went on about my business of driving home, but this event continues to haunt me to this day. I often glance in my rearview mirror and see his taunting face staring back at me in the form of an innocent stranger. Fear grips my heart and I have to blink several times to see the stranger for who they really are. It is very tiresome and angers me that he can still have any effect on my life. I was becoming more and more anxious for the week to end so that my children and I could go back to our normal life. As I arrived

home one night exhausted from a double shift with worn out feet, I instantly retreated to my bedroom in the back of the trailer. I was too tired for pleasantries and resented the fact that he was in my home. I resented the fact that he could come along
and be the hero to the kids. Here I was busting my butt trying to pay for their food,
shoes, electricity, the roof over their head, their books for school and had nothing
left over for fun. We couldn't afford to go out to eat or to go to a movie, yet he could
just waltz into town and appear to have cash to spare. It seemed unfair and I was too
tired to pretend all was ok this night. As I prepared to go to bed, he entered my room
unannounced. Startled, I looked up with a questioning look on my face. He closed
the door behind him and I began to look around for an escape. I thought at first that
he may be wanting things to get physical, in a romantic way and my mind raced for
an out. How could I get out of this situation without making him mad? This was not
his intention at all. He was angry. He accused me of not even trying to make this
work. As he raised his voice louder and louder, I saw his clenched fists and that look
come over his face that I had seen a hundred times before. His face would change
almost supernaturally and take on the form of what I could only imagine a demon
might look like. He virtually spat out words of disgust and hatred using words that
I had never heard come out of anyone's mouth directed toward me. I was frozen
with fear. I was afraid that anything I said or did would further infuriate him. As
things escalated, he was consumed further and further into an uncontrollable rage
and in an instant, he ripped the headboard off my full-size bed, knocking me on my
back with it and pinning me down by the throat. He informed me that he was going
to kill me and as I lay helplessly under the weight of both him and the headboard,
I believed it to be true. I began to pray for God to take care of my babies and to
forgive me for all I had done wrong in the hopes that I may be allowed into heaven
even though I had failed Him in so many ways. The room began to spin as I gasped
for air and started to lose consciousness. I was resolved to this end, what choice
did I have anyway? My last concerns and prayers were for that of my children. But
God had other plans. As I was slipping into unconsciousness, my oldest son at a
mere 13 years of age burst into the room. Unbeknownst to me he had been listening
all the while from the other side of the wall in his sister's room. Just like an angel,
sent from God, he began yelling at his father, distracting him enough for me to roll
out of his reach and escape out the back through the sliding glass doors beside my
bed. I ran next door to my parent's house, that place that had been the safe haven of
my childhood. My mother met me in the driveway, and I tried to catch my breath.

I recounted the events that had just unfolded next door. Her response was a simple, "You made your bed." I walked back toward my home where my children were still located along with their deranged father. During that walk home I made some decisions. I would no longer let anyone tell me I was not worth more than this. I was finished being the victim. I was finished allowing anyone else to tell me who I was or who I was going to be. The negative opinions of others would no longer define me. I ordered my husband out of the home and my children and I continued as though nothing had ever happened. I did not call the police. Looking back now, I wonder why? That seems so foolish. If someone tries to kill you, the first response would be to call 911, right? The only answer I have been able to come up with is that my mother had told me I deserved what I got so perhaps I had no right to call the authorities. Nevertheless, a line had been crossed that night and I decided that if I were not safe playing the game and waiting for him to tire of being alone, then I would do it. I would file, and the next morning I did exactly that. I began to take a firm control of my own life and my own future.

When I arrived at the courthouse the next morning, I was filled with a whirlwind of emotions. I felt ashamed of my inability to maintain my marriage, to be good enough to make him happy. I felt guilty of committing the ultimate sin of getting a divorce and breaking the covenant made before God to love, honor, and cherish this man til death do us part. I felt heartbroken that my dreams of happy-ever-after for my little family were seemingly shattered beyond repair. Most of all, I felt determined to change the direction of this life I found myself being swallowed up by. As I talked to the clerk, I was assigned legal representation and strongly advised to file a restraining order against him. This was a foreign concept for me. Someone was telling me this was not right. Granted, up to this point, the only people who knew about it were my husband, the aggressor, and my mother, who seemed determined to let me find my own way. I listened intently as I was advised that I must keep my children and myself safe and that it would be in our best interest to have some sort of record of this occurrence. They were very helpful in getting this taken care of. I silently wondered how I got to this place. I never thought I would be sitting in a courthouse with a public defender, filling out a paper to get a restraining order on my husband of 14 years. This was not the fairytale ending I had envisioned as a child for how my life would end. Little did I know, this was nowhere near the end that God had in store for me. I also found out on this day that in the state of Indiana, prior to being granted a divorce you had to undergo counseling. The point of this was to ensure that prospective divorced parents would learn to co-parent without mentally damaging their children. This counseling was much more than that to me. Yes, I learned some valuable concepts about not speaking poorly about my children's father to them and never putting them in the middle, but there was something even more important to my healing. I naively asked the counselor one day if she thought I had made the right decision in filing for a divorce. With total disbelief on her face she told me that mine was one of the worst cases of abuse she had personally ever dealt with and that I had absolutely, without a doubt made the right choice. She told me that if nothing else, I had shown my children that there are consequences for abuse. I had shown my sons that if you chose to hurt those you love, you end up sad and alone and I had shown my daughter that you do not let anyone treat you like this. This made things slightly better. Maybe I had done one thing right.

Even if the therapist believed in what I was trying to do, my parents seemingly did not. While in the process of divorce, things went from bad to worse with them. My son told me he had found a drawer at his grandma's house that contained notes she had written about me going out at night and leaving my children unattended. I thought we had an agreement that she would keep an eye on them until I returned home. She had initiated a heart to heart with me a few weeks prior, imploring me to drop out of school, go on welfare and stay home and be a mom to my kids. She thought that I could return to school after they were grown and out of the house. I thought she understood when I told her that I was doing this for them. I didn't want them to grow up thinking you don't have to work for what you get because the government will support you. I wanted to not only have money to buy them things they needed as they grew up, but I wanted to show them that they don't let what happens to them define them. I wanted them to understand that with hard work, they can do anything they wanted to do. I guess she had not listened and was still under the impression that I was simply shirking my parenting responsibilities by following my dreams of a better future for my family. My mother was from a different time. When she grew up, the mother stayed home and raised the kids. She had not gone to college and likely never even entertained the notion. She was content and fulfilled to be taken care of by a qualified husband. I think in her mind, I was an utter and total failure. I had become pregnant in high school, now was getting a divorce, worked outside of the home, leaving my poor neglected children to fend for themselves or be taken care of by their grandparents and to top it all off, was now going out to the bars and gallivanting around doing who knows what after work. All of this was more than she could wrap her mind around, and she apparently had been coming into my home when I was gone and taking things to add to her evidence against me. I never saw the drawer and am not sure what she could have found. I wasn't doing drugs or drinking alcohol and had never had any of those things in the house, but she thought she had the goods on me. In addition to this revelation, on one occasion I was walking across the yard to visit and noticed that my brother's car was in the driveway. I was excited to see that there was a party going on and I was just in time. Upon entering the house, it was obvious that I was not invited to the party and, in fact, I had interrupted a secret meeting. My mother quickly got up and removed what appeared to me to be some sort of scanner and before I was spotted, I heard conversation about listening in on my phone conversations. You see, back in the day, scanners could pick up cordless telephone conversations. With tears in my eyes, I confronted my family about what I already knew to be true. My father lied to me and said it wasn't, but I already knew. I was hurt beyond belief. When asked what they were trying to accomplish with the spying, rifling through my belongings and accumulating the goods on me, my mother told me they were thinking about trying to get my kids taken away. Not that they wanted them, that would have been bad enough, but what followed was even worse. She told me that she believed they would be better off with their father than with me. They would be better off with a man who beat them, degraded them, and spent all of his money on women rather than supply their needs. My mother has since told me she never wanted to send the kids back to their dad, so perhaps those words were said out of a desperate attempt to control the situation, but at the time, I didn't know this. I believed that my own mother thought so poorly of me that, in her mind, this would be a better option for them. Heartbroken once again, I walked that walk across the yard to my trailer. I unplugged the wireless phone and began making plans to move away from my so-called family. Before long I found a home for rent in a neighboring town for a reasonable price. It was a large farmhouse and was a bit run down, but was, by far, a better option in my mind than being beholden in any way to my parents who were not understanding of my situation. We were now totally on our own. No grandparents next door to help and no husband. It was my children and me and we forged a mighty team as we trudged onward into our ever frightening and uncertain future.

I found myself glaringly alone when the day finally arrived, I was to go to court for the ruling on the divorce. My husband didn't show up and this seemed to infuriate the judge. I was granted everything my lawyer asked for. I received full custody of the children along with child support, which I would never receive. As we left the courtroom I felt utterly dragged down with grief. My lawyer looked quizzically at me and said, "You look like you lost or something. You should be ecstatic." I explained that there is nothing happy about divorce. I never wanted my life to go this way. I wanted the happily ever after and this was more like the death of my dream than a celebration. I could find nothing to smile about.

As if I were not beat down enough, school was tough. I had always felt that I was smart and good at this school thing, but no longer. The course work in the program was difficult, intense, and plentiful. The program schedule was planned out for you and it varied from 15 to 18 credit hours per semester. These were not cake classes either, rather they were classes like Kinesiology, Neuroanatomy, and Common Medical Conditions. I tried so hard to read all the assigned readings but, with my schedule, this proved to be an impossible feat. It went against everything that was within me to not do what was assigned to me, but I simply had no other option. I learned to scan the readings, highlighting what I believed to be important and use that, along with the lecture notes, to study for the tests. For the first time in my life, I developed test anxiety. I would become physically ill, spending a portion of the test time in the bathroom. In high school, there was nothing riding on the tests other than my parent's disapproval, but here, my children's future was on the line. If I dropped below an 87% in any one class, I would be kicked out of the program. Everything I had done so far, would be for nothing. I could not let that happen. I had to succeed, no matter what. I pushed myself harder than ever before toward this goal to the point of becoming almost obsessed with the idea of showing my kids that we would not be determined by our past. We would instead be whomever we decided we would be.

Then came the class that threatened to end it all, Common Medical Conditions. This was a three-hour class with a guest speaker who was an expert in his or her particular field. For instance, an oncologist came to speak on cancer, an endocrinologist came to speak about diabetes and a gastroenterologist came to speak about stomach disorders. This was all very fine and dandy except, most of these leaders in their field did not speak in normal people language. I can remember sitting through class one day when we had three different specialists, each speaking for one hour on their area of expertise and at the end they asked if anyone had any questions.

My question was, "What?" It was all such a blur that I could not even formulate an intelligent question. The class had only three tests through the entire semester and I somehow managed to glean enough information from the myriad of specialists to pass the first one with an A. The second test was over prescription medication. During this portion of lecture, we learned about brand name drugs, generic name drugs, their uses, their side effects, and their contraindications. There was so much information that I had no idea how to study. I knew there was no way to learn it all. There was simply too much information to memorize. I had to decide which part of this information I was going to focus on, and I chose wrong. I studied one thing and the test was on another and I failed it. I was devastated. I met with my instructor and was told in order to remain eligible for the program I would have to score no less than a 91% on the final test of the class. The next few weeks were a blur as I tried to be sure I knew everything that could possibly be included in that test. In the end, I aced it with a 98%. I am not sure how, but I certainly was glad. I could now continue on my journey toward a better life.

It became me and my children against the world. We were a strong unit and we believed that together we could get through anything. As I trudged along with attempting to juggle work at Red Lobster, college studies and raising three kids on my own, my children were facing struggles of their own. I will have to admit that I barely noticed. If I really thought about it, I felt too guilty, so I pushed it to the back of my mind. I was never there to wake them up in the mornings and to see them off to school. My 8-year-old daughter set her alarm early and saw to it that her brothers caught the school bus. I was never available to go on class field trips because I was in Indianapolis attending class myself. I was never there to greet them when they got off the school bus. Whether their day was good or whether it was bad, I was unavailable for them to talk to me about it. I was never there to make dinner for them. Once again this fell to my 8-year-old daughter. Laundry, if it was to be washed, was again up to Whitney. An 8-year-old became the acting mother of the house. Looking back, I now can see that at times her brothers didn't appreciate being mothered by her. Occasionally when I arrived home, I would find that Whitney had barricaded herself in her room saying that her brothers were being mean to her. She never elaborated. I took it to mean that they were teasing her, but I had no time to investigate.

Money was tight. I took out the max amount of student loans I could get every semester to make sure I could pay for everything we would need to get by. I could consistently anticipate $300 per week from Red Lobster but that didn't stretch very far. As for the child support that was ordered, in total I saw a whopping $78 in the form of one payment. When I went to the court to see what they were doing about the monthly amount not coming through their system, I was informed that he was out of state and claiming disability and that there was nothing they could do about it. It seemed so messed up that a man could drive a race car every weekend while claiming disability, but no one was interested in my opinion. I was on my own and over time would come to find that this only served to make the victory sweeter.

Raising three children on my own was challenging, and not just financially. It was tough mentally as well. I never knew if I was being too tough or too easy when I made a decision. I was always second guessing myself. I tried to be a good mom but often it seemed that I just wasn't enough. One evening, after barricading myself in my room for the night to study, my daughter Whitney knocked on my door. I wondered why she was up. She should have been asleep by then. She told me that I needed to go outside to check on Monty because something was wrong with him. I quickly ran to see what was wrong and he was standing out in our driveway, baseball bat in hand, wailing on a telephone pole. He was beating it over and over and yelling at it. He was nearly hoarse and I wondered how long he had been doing this. As I got closer, I could make out what he was saying. He was talking to the telephone pole as if it were his dad. He was saying, "Go ahead, just try to hit me now. You think you are such a big man." He was out of his head and not responding to my voice. I cautiously approached him and touched his shoulder which thankfully brought him back to reality. As I took the bat from his hands the magnitude of this moment was crystal clear. The blood dripped from his hands, where blisters had formed and then ripped open as he repeatedly hit the bat against the pole. He had so much anger toward his dad. What had this man done to my baby? I did the only thing I knew to do. I held him and loved him. I told him he never had to be afraid of his dad hurting him again. In hindsight, I wish I would have taken him to counseling to help him make sense of all the hurt that was in his head and in his heart, but I didn't. I didn't know what was available and I had no one to help me. I was alone, raising three kids and was trying my best to make right this horrible wrong that had been done to them, but I was severely unqualified for the job. My children needed a father they couldn't have.

Homecoming 2002 Whitney had just been crowned Duchess. Monty sophomore, Chad freshman, and Whitney 7th grade

10
MOVING FORWARD

I knew my children needed a father in their lives. Even so, it didn't make it easy when summer rolled around, and it was time for their court ordered two-week summer visitation. I couldn't help but be concerned. It was scary sending them off with him for two whole weeks without me there to protect them, but I firmly believed he would be on his best behavior. After all, Chad had only recently agreed to having anything to do with him. Prior to that, he had refused all attempts made by his father to have a relationship with him. My now ex-husband, made travel arrangements and my children were off to Florida for two weeks. After a week went by, I contacted him to find out when they would be arriving back home, and he said that he had no money to return them. I am not sure why this surprised me because it was pretty much par for the course with him but I, being a single mom, working 3 days at Red Lobster and raising 3 kids with no financial assistance from their father, didn't have it either. I managed to scrounge up enough to fly them home but when they arrived there were only two. My oldest was not with them. When talking to him over the phone, he informed me that he would be staying in Florida to live with his dad. He maintained that it was not fair to his dad to have to be all alone and that he knew I would be alright because I had his brother and sister. I was not alright.

was worried sick. There was no way this man who was physically abusive to his children, had changed and would now provide a safe and loving environment for his son. He had gotten remarried, to a woman with two children from a previous marriage and Monty would be living with them. This was what he wanted. What could I do about it? I was incredibly hurt. How could this child not remember why we left? Did he forget why I had made the difficult decision to take my children, leaving our home and all our belongings and flee the state? Did he also forget the night his father had attempted to kill me, and he had to step in? The communication between us fell silent. I could never reach him by phone and no attempts at reaching me were being made. Finally, one night at 3 a.m. my phone rang. It was Monty and he was crying. Through whispers he told me that he was being mistreated. He said they would not let him use the phone to call me, so he had to sneak and do it when they were asleep. He also told me they wouldn't buy him anything. He said he was hungry and had no clothes or shoes that fit his ever-growing feet. He said his dad had not changed and was just as mean as ever but now his anger was also directed towards his new step kids. As I pondered what to do with this new predicament, the late-night phone calls kept us connected. There was no communication with my ex as he continued to ignore my calls, but he had managed to use my son's information to get additional government assistance for his family. I continued to work every chance I had and attempted to somehow put together enough money to bring Monty home. Little did I know that this was not something I would need to make happen.

The events that would transpire to bring my son home began one night, in the middle of my shift at Red Lobster when the manager called me aside and told me there was a call for me. This was strange, as no one ever called me at work. It was the police. My heart began to beat wildly out of my chest as I tried desperately to make sense out of what they were saying. They told me there had been a wreck involving my son Chad. He was alive but was taken by ambulance to Ball Memorial Hospital. I immediately raced to my car and began the long drive from Richmond to Muncie. I called Whitney and Monty on the way to let them know what was happening. Whitney pleaded with me to come by and pick her up. It was not out of the way, so I instructed her to be by the road and jump in the car as soon as I arrived. Little did I know that by driving to Muncie by way of my house, it would take us upon the site of the wreck. If my fear level was not high enough, it was pushed over the edge when I saw the mangled mess of a pickup truck and a van near an intersection along the road. I knew immediately this was the accident Chad

had been involved in and after seeing the aftermath was even more afraid for him. Upon arriving at the hospital, we were ushered into the emergency department and found Chad laying on a backboard with a neck brace and a bandage covering his side. All the resolve to be brave melted away at the sight of his mother and tears began streaming down Chad's face. He was trying to reach out to me but was sternly warned by the doctor that he was not to move a muscle. I was advised that Chad had been ejected through the windshield of his friend Brett's truck when Brett ran a stop sign and they slammed directly into the side of a minivan. On the way out of the truck, a dagger of broken glass caught his side and ripped a hole in him that, in the end, required three layers of stiches. The surgeon reported that he had repaired gunshot wounds that were less severe. The fear was that the glass may have done damage to his internal organs and tests would need to be run. He also had a gash on his head that would require 14 staples and was wearing a neck brace until it could be determined if any vertebrae were broken as he exited the vehicle or as he landed in the field 500 feet away. Miraculously, there was no internal head injury and no injury to his organs. Chad would later tell me why my little rule follower did not have a seat belt on. He was headed to Muncie with his older friend Brett and they decided to turn back to the house to retrieve Chad's CDs. They were in a rush to get to the store before it closed so after running in the house he jumped into the truck, CDs in hand and they sped off. In the excitement, he had forgotten to put the seat belt back on. A mistake for which he paid dearly.

Monty who was more than 900 miles away could hardly stand not being with his brother. He begged his father to drive him back to Indiana, but Brandon had other priorities and refused to make the trip until after the weekend races. For Monty, this would be the last straw. He had stayed in Florida with his father because he felt sorry for him. He was all alone, with no one to love him but this situation spoke loud and clear to Monty. His father was alone because he selfishly only cared for himself. He appeared unconcerned for his youngest son and that was not ok with Monty. Chad and Monty had an amazing bond from an early age. That bond was more important to Monty than anything. When his dad finally brought him back to Indiana, he boldly broke the news to him that he would not be returning to Florida with him. He would be staying here with his brother. When I saw Monty, I was overcome with emotion. He was finally back. When I saw his tattered shoes that were at least 2 sizes too small, it broke my heart. What was wrong with this man, this so called "dad?" Why would he not make sure his own flesh and blood had everything he needed? Monty had been given the shoes on his feet by a friend. They didn't fit but they were all he had. I was furious with his father for taking money from the government for my child and then not even providing his basic needs. Money for me was tight but we went the following day and bought my son shoes that fit his feet. With my family back intact, I continued to press on toward my goal of being able to support them.

Finally, I finished my schooling and graduated. My parents and children were all there to see it. As I looked at the huge smiles that crossed their faces as they all beamed with pride, I realized that I had done it. I had shown my children that they don't have to just take what life throws at them. They do not have to be victims of their circumstance. When life knocks them down, they can choose to get back up again stronger than ever before. My parents and I never again spoke of the strain that had driven a wedge in between us. We just slowly began acting as though nothing had never happened. At this point, I mistakenly thought I was the one in control of my life. After the mess I had found myself in, I had decided to take control of my life and to stop letting life happen to me. I had become calloused and strong. I took my life back and I had done it. I remember my mother asking me one day, "Don't you think God had something to do with it?" I stored that somewhere in the back of my mind but took offense to her comment and determined that she was, once again, minimizing my own struggle and hard work. I had done this. I had sacrificed. I had stayed up late studying and working on very little sleep. I had learned the material. I had made the grades. I had gone deep into debt. I had done it. I still believed in God but trusted in me because I was the one who got up and took control and did something about my circumstance. If I had sat around and waited on God to do something, I reasoned that I would likely be dead, certainly not where I was now. I had prayed to God for years to fix my life and He seemingly didn't care, didn't listen and didn't move…or did He? What I didn't realize then was that God's hand was all over my life gently steering and guiding me back to a place where He could not only use me but bless me beyond belief.

While I was juggling to get everything in place to begin our new life, my now 13-year old daughter was beginning to want some independence. She had been repeatedly told that she would be able to start dating when she turned 16 but she didn't like that answer. An older boy, with a car had begun pursuing her and this was exciting and flattering to a 7th grader. She had always been such a rule follower that it came as quite the surprise that while sitting on the bleachers at her brother's track meet, I overheard a friend ask her if she had fun the night before. She attempted to silence her friend but it was too late. I perked up immediately, straining intently to listen in on this private conversation. Upon returning home, I questioned her about what had been said. She hesitantly admitted to sneaking out of her window after I had gone to sleep to go out with this older boy. Her two big brothers overheard our conversation and immediately went to have a talk with this misguided young lad, who would never attempt this misstep again. I was so thankful she had these two to protect her, although I did sympathize with her, as news traveled throughout our community of her protectors and no boy wanted to come against them. Even if she had no father to look out for her, she had her brothers, whether she liked it or not.

The next step for my career, was to apply for a temporary OT license. After finishing all the required classwork and fieldwork, I could work as a real OT while studying for my final licensing test. I thought that by working and applying the things I had learned, it may help me pass that dreaded test. I began by walking into every facility within 30 minutes of my home and asking if they needed an OT. After striking out three times I stumbled upon a nursing home and walked directly into the building administrator's office, resume in hand. The administrator asked me quizzically, how I knew they needed an OT. He read through my resume and was thoroughly impressed. He went on and on about how wonderful I seemed to be. I skeptically smiled and thought, this man is either an idiot, a liar or I am a really good writer, because all that I have done is be a lousy wife, a struggling mother and pretty good student, but if he wanted to be impressed, so be it.

I got the job working under another OTR and my pay quickly went from $2.13 an hour to $25 an hour, with the promise of a raise when I was fully licensed. When I was taking my classes I often felt overwhelmed by the workload and wondered if any of this was sticking in my brain. It was so much to learn but as I began to work and apply my knowledge, I was happy to learn that it had stuck. I did remember this stuff. With each new patient and each new diagnosis, my schooling would come back to me. This was great! Maybe I could do this. At lunch that first day, I sat at my desk amazed that they were paying me to do this. This was so much easier than waiting on unhappy Red Lobster patrons and I had already made as much in half a day as I would have normally made working a double shift at the restaurant. I had made the right choice in finishing my schooling. Don't misunderstand, everything was not sunshine and roses. My new supervisor was a man from Nigeria, and he had a chip on his shoulder about his new subordinate. He felt I was less than him and he made sure to make that clear every chance he got. Back in those days, everything was done with paper and pen so each evaluation I completed was sure to be rejected by him and sent back for me to redo. I am a perfectionist by nature so I was sure I was completing everything exactly as it should be but, none the less, he would determine I had measured something wrong or misstated something and would make me rewrite the entire evaluation. I resented his condescending glances and snide remarks but still this was better than the server gig. My new job would not result in a paycheck for 3 weeks since they held the first paycheck and I started a week into the first pay period. Because of this, I had to continue working at Red Lobster on the weekends for 3 weeks as I worked through the week as a therapist. Red Lobster became harder and harder to bear. Throughout the week, I was getting the respect of doctors as they asked for my opinion as to whether their patient was ready to return home but then, on the weekends, I was getting disrespected by high school dropouts because I didn't get their salads to them quick enough. I remember thinking, you have no idea who I am, what I have come through or what I will be doing next week, yet you choose to think I am worthy of your disrespect simply because I am a server. No one deserves to be disrespected simply for trying to support her family. I began counting down the days until I would no longer have to run myself ragged, trying to please crabby, malcontented guests of which there was no pleasing.

The day finally arrived when I got my first real paycheck. I was standing at the nurse's desk with the nurses and CNAs as we all opened our paychecks. I had carefully figured my pay and was looking forward to getting a $1000 paycheck from that first week of work. When I opened it, the amount was far less than I expected. As I scanned the entire document, I quickly surmised why this had happened... taxes. Before I thought it through, I expressed my surprise aloud exclaiming, "They took over $300 for taxes?" My question immediately elicited a question by the closest CNA of "How much do you make?" She then stated that what they took out of my check in taxes was far more than her entire check. I quickly checked myself and vowed never to make that mistake again. I should be thankful that I now had the ability to earn enough money to warrant the government taking that much out in taxes. Still it didn't seem fair. I was the one who worked for that. I would just have to keep that disappointment to myself as I moved on toward securing a future for my family.

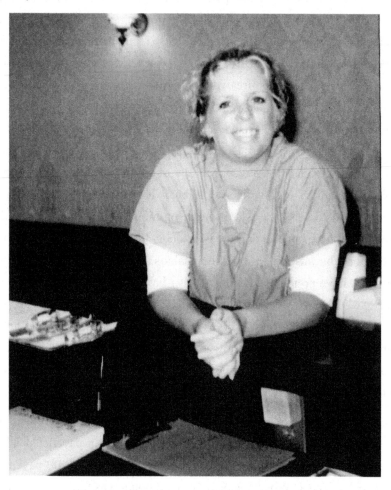

Me at my first job as an OT

I scheduled my Occupational Therapy Boards for March of that year and had mixed feelings about this upcoming mile marker. It would be great to get that $1 er hour raise I had been promised upon passing and I foolishly thought that having my license might gain me a little respect from my misogynistic mentor. Whether I ever received respect from him, my work would no longer have to be approved by him, so things were bound to be better. On the other hand, I despised tests. They stressed me out immensely. I could feel the anxiety welling up inside me as that fateful date in March drew near. My days were spent at the nursing home completing hands on learning and my evenings were spent with my head in the books, desperately attempting to decipher exactly what I was supposed to know, out of this immense sea of facts that I had been given throughout the program. Studying when you have 3 children is not an easy task. They wanted my attention. They wanted me to look at their schoolwork, to attend their sporting events, to be there. I found myself torn, trying desperately to be everything to everybody while preparing to take the biggest test of my life. If I failed, I would be fired. I would no longer have my $25 per hour job. Everything I had worked so hard for over the past five years would be for naught. I knew Red Lobster would welcome me back but failing was not an option. I had to pass this test. My children's futures were depending on it. The evening before my test, in an attempt to limit last minute distractions and to minimize the chance that I would be late to the exam, I asked my mom to watch the kids and I drove to Indianapolis and got a hotel room. I then drove to the test site, to ensure I knew where to go, before hunkering down in my room, studying and praying. It was all so overwhelming and as the anxiety and the heaviness of this moment threatened to overtake me, I realized that if I didn't already know it, I wasn't going to learn it tonight. I finally fell asleep knowing my time of preparation was over. It was now time to certify that I was competent to be trusted as an Occupational Therapist. The next morning, I awoke early, feeling refreshed and ready to put this fear and anxiety behind me. As I arrived at the testing site, I could hardly breath. My head and stomach were swirling as I asked the proctor where I could find the restroom and if I would be able to utilize it during the test if necessary. In the end, it had not been necessary as I became totally immersed in the test. I quickly ascertained that this was not your normal test. Each question had 4 answers. One was wrong, that was the easy part, one was the correct answer, then there were two that were partially correct. There were many about what would you do when presented with this patient. This seemed crazy. I had worked in a nursing home for the past several months and I knew that along with each new patient, came a whole set of new facts. One diagnosis did not set the course of treatment. There were many factors that came into play including medical diagnosis, patient goals, family, resources, mental status and the list goes on and on. How was I to know what the writer of each question thought was the correct response? It was all so subjective. I answered each question with what I would have done if the case presented itself in the clinic and left that day having no clue if I passed or failed. All that was left to do was wait, pray and hope for the best. It was now out of my control. Surprisingly, I found that I liked that there was no more for me to do. I had been working so hard to control the outcome but now I could finally rest. Studying and stressing would do nothing for me now. The days dragged on as I anxiously checked my mail each day as I returned home from work. When the letter finally arrived, my hands were trembling as I struggled to open the envelope. I held my breath and read the first line, "The National Board for Certification in Occupational Therapy congratulates you on the successful completion of your certification requirements…" It was over. I had passed. I had done it. Now it was time to get on with my life.

Getting on with my life was a challenge in itself. I couldn't get a loan on my own, due to my past financial situation, but I found that with my dad co-signing, I could buy my very first new car. I bought a base model Chevrolet, but it was mine and it was new. I could finally quit driving the gas guzzler that my grandmother had so graciously given me. Things were indeed looking up. I was able to easily pay my monthly bills and take care of my children. We had gone without for so long that I foolishly spent every dime I made. It felt nice to be able to buy my son that game he wanted or to buy my daughter that extra pair of shoes she was eyeing. I now know that you do not do your children any favors by ensuring that they want for nothing. You are merely giving them the feeling of entitlement. Gratitude and appreciation are nurtured by having to work and earn those extra wants. But I was young and trying to raise these kids on my own, so this was just one of my many mistakes. We moved out of the rundown farmhouse, which was soon after condemned and torn down, and moved up to a fancy new apartment in a nearby town. I bought all new furniture. I bought everything my little heart desired.

Another upside of my new career was that I never had to miss another of my children's ballgames. They played everything and there was nothing I liked better than watching them play. Their father had pretty much dropped off the face of the earth. After a couple of halfhearted attempts at planning to come see them, his interest became less and less. I preferred it that way. I didn't know how many more times I could bear to drag Monty in from the side of the road where he was sitting in front of our house with his suitcase because his dad had promised he would come, but never showed. It seemed to me that it was more hurtful to them to be disappointed in him than to have no interaction with him. I did the best I could and loved them with everything inside of me, all the while hoping I could somehow love them enough to make up for the giant void that a father is supposed to fill. There I was alone, but at every ballgame cheering them on and relishing every moment. They were so much fun to watch. On the outside it seemed they were doing well. I had no idea what was really going on until a caring coach requested a meeting.

I remember being asked to come in and speak to the high school basketball coach concerning my younger son Chad. The coach was expressing his frustration with his inability to get Chad to listen to him. He said it would all be fine one minute, but as soon as he tried to push him, to get more from him, Chad seemed to tune him out. I asked what tactic he was using to challenge or push him. The coach told me he typically would get in his face and yell. He said when he did that, he got absolutely no response from him. In fact, Chad would just begin to stare straight ahead and act as though he wasn't listening. I fought back the tears as I explained Chad's history to the coach. I explained that his father would beat him and scream in his face and because of that, when faced with a situation that feels dangerous Chad shuts down. It almost seems like he leaves the situation mentally in order to survive. I was certain he had learned this when being abused earlier in life. By the time I finished explaining, we were both in tears. The coach had no idea about Chad's past. No one did. I thought it best to keep it quiet, in order to protect the kids. Perhaps that was a mistake. From that day forward the coach found a gentler approach to getting more from my son but I couldn't follow my child through life explaining the damage that had been done by his father. I hoped he would learn to adjust and live a happy productive life. Guilt overwhelmed me. How had I allowed this abuse for so long? My son was dependent on me to keep him safe and I had failed. If you can't trust your mom, who can you trust? How could I ever make this right? I mistakenly thought that the answer to remedy the situation was in finding a new father figure for my children.

11

LEARNING CURVE

had begun dating again while working at Red Lobster but the places I had been meeting men were not generating anything of quality, still the diversion was nice. It was a welcome change to have something or someone new to think about. It was flattering to have a man tell me how pretty I was or how much he liked me. It had been many years since I had been on the dating scene and things sure had changed. As a 17-year-old in 1983, sometimes a guy may get a little fresh on a date but there were really no expectations of anything happening. Now at 34 years old in 2001, times sure had changed. It appeared that sex was now an expectation. As a woman who believed that sex outside of marriage was wrong, it was so frustrating to find that the twenty-first century man seemed to have quite the opposing viewpoint. Finding someone to ask me out was not difficult. However, finding someone of high caliber would prove to be very difficult. I went out with a construction worker I met at Wendy's, but he ended up having a wife and child. I hung out with an attractive man I met at the Speedway gas station, but after going missing for days on end with no explanation, I discovered that he was addicted to cocaine. I thought it was a bit strange that his pinky fingernail was longer than mine, but naïve me had no idea what he might be growing it for. I was courted by an ex-stripper whom I met at the mall whose idea of a first date, and last by the way, was to go to the strip club to watch his buddies dance. I was mortified. This was nothing like the romantic notion I had of Chippendale dancers. You know the image, extremely attractive, well-built men in cute costumes, dancing sexily around in unison. Oh no, I was in for a shock. This was dirty, nasty, grinding, make you want to go home and shower with disinfectant soap for hours, stripping. Luckily, my tactic of slouching down, way back in the corner and refusing to make eye contact, successfully worked as a repellant to these cockroaches and not one of them chose me for a special dance. If they had, I surely would have died. Out of the half open corner of one eye, I saw what one of them did to one poor girl and it bordered on assault. There was nothing sexy or romantic about it. One by one, every guy I went out with ended up being not what I was looking for. This dating thing was not working out so well.

I began contemplating my options. I had grown tired of the bar scene. There really is no compliment in a drunk guy thinking you are attractive. I had met these men at the gas station, at the mall, at restaurants but they were all the same and not of the quality I wanted as an example for my children. Not only that, but they were also beginning to bore me. They had no larger ambitions than to see how far they could get with me. I knew I wanted to find a good Christian man but there were no single men in church. To me it seemed that everyone was coupled up in church. Everyone was sitting with their spouse and their family and then there I was, the outcast. The divorced woman sitting with no partner feeling as if I had a scarlet letter on my chest. Luckily, my children would go to church with me, but I still felt like the outlier. There was no one else like me there, only people with seemingly perfect lives. My life still felt like a mess. In an attempt to intellectually figure out how to secure a partner for me, I read every self-help book I could find and following the advice in one, I made a list of the top ten qualities I wanted in a man.

Things I want in a man

1. Christian
2. Trust worthy
3. Intelligent
4. Funny
5. Ambitious
6. Chemistry
7. Treats me kind
8. Shows me respect
9. Fit
10. Confidant

Top ten list

It did not go unnoticed by me that my top ten qualities in a man were pretty much all opposites of my former choice for a companion. I tucked this list away in the book and continued my quest to find a companion for me and a role model for my children. I finally settled upon the online dating scene to strategically find the man for me. Online, you could explicitly detail what you were looking for and screen the potential candidates carefully by painstakingly going through every detail in their profile. Next, you could chat online to get a feel for their character safely from afar. If they passed that test, you could chat with them on the phone and get an idea if there was any connection. This seemed much safer to me than picking someone up in the mall. I could drop them as soon as I found a flaw and didn't have to see that sad look in their eyes. I didn't even have to listen to their sad pleas that they would wait for me forever to change my mind because I could just block them, and it was done. I signed up for multiple dating sites and it became quite the game. This was a fun, safe, no commitment way to feel wanted. Every night I would come home from work and could flirt with my most recent candidates, or not. I was in control and I liked it that way. The problem was, as I began choosing to meet them in person, I found out something that shocked me. People lie. Time after time I would meet someone who turned out to not be who they claimed to be. The things I learned dating online can be summed up this way. If they don't have a profile picture, there is a reason and that reason is not that they can't get their photo to upload to the site. If they are wearing a hat, they have no hair. Saying they are single does not guarantee they are not married. Saying they make a good income does not necessarily mean they are employed. Displaying a picture of a fancy hot rod as their vehicle does not mean that their true mode of transportation is not a moped.

Early on I had connected with a man who told me he had been told his best quality was his smile. He said he drove a red Camaro and eventually we decided to meet. He was coming from a couple of hours away, so we agreed we would get together in between in a public place. He said he would call me when he was leaving his house sometime after five pm. I was all dressed and ready to go by five, but there was no call. Finally, he called around seven, apologized for being so late and pleaded with me to follow through on our plans. This was strike one. I hesitantly agreed to still meet, but when he suggested McDonalds, I gave him a firm no. His choice of romantic meeting spots was strike two. I arrived first at the alternate location of Pizza Hut and chose to remain in my car until he arrived in his red Camaro. When he pulled up in an old white box van and exclaimed, "You are not going to believe this, but my Camaro wouldn't start!" He was right, I didn't believe it, strike three. He was out before we even got in the restaurant, but I didn't want to be rude, so I decided to continue with the ruse. As I sat across from the man wearing his matching NASCAR hat and jacket I softly whispered to myself, "You can do this," but then he smiled. Whoever told him he had a beautiful smile was not only dishonest but a bit cruel. That was not how I would have described it. The date only went downhill from there. When the waitress arrived to take our orders, he announced that he wanted nothing, he had already eaten. He went on to explain that the reason he was so late was his ex-wife had offered to buy him dinner and he never passed up a free meal. Let me tell you, I am very good at controlling what my mouth says, but have never been able to control what my face says. So, that being said, I think he could tell he was losing me. Just when I thought it couldn't get any worse, it did. In one last ditch effort to impress me he asked if I wanted to see his tattoos. Before I could even get the word, "No" out of my mouth, he ripped off his jacket and white t-shirt right there in the middle of the Pizza Hut. I was mortified as I slunk down as low into the booth as I could in the hopes that no one would see me with this simpleton. I continued to eat my pizza as he sat bare chested across from me, proudly displaying his body art. I couldn't get out of there fast enough. I quickly finished my dinner and he walked me to the car. Somehow, I guess he missed my nonverbals and came in for the kiss. I skillfully dodged it and slid into my car quickly closing the door. He promised to call, but I blocked his number as soon as he got in his work van. He did not meet my top ten qualities and was especially lacking with regards to #2 and #3, trustworthy and intelligent. I made a mental note that no profile picture in the future, meant no date with me.

I made sure the next connection had a profile picture. After chatting for a while, he invited me to come to his home at Geist Reservoir, an upscale community near me. I could hear the voice in my head telling me it is not wise to go to his home, but the intrigue of seeing what a fancy house in that neighborhood looked like overcame my reservations and I agreed. On the determined night, I excitedly pulled into a neighborhood that I had never even imagined. All the houses were grand and the address my GPS took me to was no exception. I was filled with excitement, as I pulled in the drive. This house was beautiful. Maybe this date would be different. I had such high hopes until he opened the door. I must have mistakenly stopped at the wrong house. This was not the man in the photo online. Once again, my face surely gave me away and he began to explain that he knows his looks have changed, but that was due to him contracting lock jaw. It felt so surreal, I recognized his voice from talking to him on the phone, but this was not the right face and I was pretty sure lockjaw did not do that, but even if it did, his profile picture should depict what he looked like now. We toured this majestic home and as I looked around everything was top notch. Even his coasters screamed of wealth, but then there were the pictures of the man online. The man I thought I was meeting. I began to formulate an understanding of the situation in my mind. This was not the man in the picture, but I believe the house belonged to the man in the picture. Who then, was this man leading me around the mansion? He must have been house sitting. Maybe he was staying there, taking care of the house and had hacked into this other man's Match. com account and had pretended to be him. Either way, I had driven a long way and was going to get something out of it. I let this stranger take me to dinner then feigned an emergency at home and cut out early. This con artist failed to pass my top ten quality list as well, failing miserably with quality #2, being trustworthy.

As I drove home, I wondered why people who lie would ever meet someone in person. Did they not know the gig would be up? It was an exciting time, none the less, as I traveled and met a wide variety of men. There was the airline pilot who looked like he could be my child, the quite likely married body builder who wouldn't let me come to his house. I eventually forgot about my list and determined that I would have to settle. I must have too high of standards for myself. That man on my list simply didn't exist.

Then I met Mick. He claimed to be a Christian. In fact, he had ambitions of becoming a preacher. He read the Bible, aloud. In fact, he did this every time we were together, which seemed a bit odd. He also prayed majestically before meals as if he were King James himself. He did look good. I had met him on the bodybuilding dating site I was on and he didn't disappoint in the fitness department, the thing was, he wasn't very smart. If he never spoke, and all I had to do was look at him, I think it may have worked out but he liked to hear himself speak. He also liked to hear himself sing, even when he didn't know the words. I tried hard to make this one work but eventually his deficits with #3 (intelligence) on my list were just too much for me to overcome. I ended it with Mick, but he was unable to gracefully let me go. He became obsessed, calling me incessantly, insisting that we were meant to be together. One morning as I was leaving for work, I found a single red rose frozen to my car. I knew he had been at my house the night before, stalking, lurking in the shadows and I began to fear him. That was not normal behavior. After a couple of weeks had gone by, a limousine pulled up at my work. The driver was carrying a dozen red roses with a note attached that said "Always." She had been hired by Mick and given a recording, with instructions to drive me around and play the recording as we drove. She admitted that she had listened to the recording on the way to my workplace and her advice was to "run because this guy is unstable." This added to my uneasiness about him and I wondered how I would ever get him to give up. The more he persisted, the less attractive I found him. Then one Saturday afternoon, he showed up to my house with his little girl. I had grown to love his daughter and thought surely, he would not do anything too crazy with her there. He wanted to talk and as we stood in the kitchen, he pinned me up against the wall and planted a big kiss on my repulsed lips. Afterward he turned on his heels, looked at his daughter and said, "There Katie, Daddy got closure!", and they were off, never to be seen again. It seemed quality #3 (intelligence) was going to be a must-have for me. I considered adding a #11 of "Not psycho," but never did.

The older my children got, the more desperate I got to find that man to stand in as a father to them. How were they supposed to learn how to be men with no male role model in their lives? That fear was not exactly warranted. They had my dad. He was the best role model a boy could ever hope to have. Sure, he made mistakes as we all do, but he was a god-fearing man who was gentle, soft spoken, kind and loving. He had a way of making me feel smart, pretty, loved and like I was his favorite person ever. He was the one who had taught me how to dream. I remember as a kid, we regularly would walk together out to the field behind our barn. The field had long been vacated by the cattle we had raised but if you looked closely you could still see the remnant depressions left by their hooves. When one looked at this abandoned field, they may not see much but my daddy did. He saw something he had always dreamed of. As he told me of his ambition to one day have a pond of his own, stocked full of bass large enough to bend the stoutest of poles, his dream became so vivid I could almost see it. He would then walk me around to what he hoped would one day be the perimeter of his pond, placing broken sticks into the ground as an outline. Years later, when I was off and married, he had made that dream a reality and built the most beautiful pond I had ever seen, complete with an island which was home to a tree and a bench to sit on, made accessible by a simple bridge.

My dad's dream come true

My dad was the reason I believed my dream could come true. He was the reason I believed I could overcome my circumstances. Maybe he could be their example. But I still felt compelled to continue my search. It became somewhat of a quest, a quest to find a new father for my children. I think this urgency led me to many poor choices as I disregarded my list and tried to reason away deficiencies. I started to think if I could only find someone who met maybe seven out of the ten criteria, I could live with that. But which three could I live without. Therein lies the rub.

My next suiter was another man from the fitness dating site. You'd think I would have learned, but apparently not. When I first met this man, I was not impressed with his looks. He was fit, but not so easy on the eyes. As had become my usual, I would just get through the date and then dump him. I disregarded the red flags that were loudly waving at me throughout the evening, one of which being that he had forgotten his wallet and I had to pay. Yet by the end of the night I had kind of been won over by his charisma. After all, none of them were perfect. There was some-

hing wrong with all of them and he was fun. Maybe I could hang out with him for
a season. He stated that he was a builder of homes and owned his own business but
because of the effects of 9/11 his business was failing, and he was struggling. He
claimed to be doing odd jobs for people who had hail damage on their roofs. After
hanging around too long, I began to care for him. He doted on me and talked of
marriage and a life together. Believing his lies, I agreed to buy a house together. But
after we moved in, he changed. He became mean, jealous and suspicious. He would
accuse me of all kinds of improprieties with vulgar expletives. I remember vividly
saying to myself, I don't have to put up with this. I do not deserve to be talked to or
treated like this and there is no marriage license holding me here. As I began to plan
my escape things only got worse. He threatened to beat up my aging father, stole
$1500 from my checking account and stashed needles and illegal steroids in my at-
tic. I came to believe the way he was truly getting his money was by selling drugs. I
secretly opened a bank account, secured a house in another town and began plotting
my escape. Even though he had threatened to kill me and anyone who helped me if
I ever attempted to leave him, I believed I could do it covertly. He would leave for
two weeks at a time on "business," whatever that meant, so I planned that the next
time he left, I would take my children and be gone when he returned. We did as I
had planned, and I held my breath as I knew he was figuring out that something was
up when I quit answering his calls. He became enraged, calling me every few minutes and texting obscenities and I wondered how I had been so stupid to ever give
this man a chance. I knew that he could find me because he knew where I worked
so I instructed the people at work to say I no longer worked there. I don't know if
he believed the lies or if he just really didn't care enough to question them, but he
eventually stopped calling. I vowed to never again ignore those red flags. I knew
I deserved more than this. I almost let us fall under the control of yet another unfit
man. I had to do more to protect my children from the evils of this world.

Unfortunately, no matter how hard you try you can't protect your children from
everything and this came fully apparent on the day when my oldest son Monty
came to me scared but excited. He told me that his high school girlfriend was pregnant. I was determined to handle this better than my parents had. I thought I had
done everything I needed to prevent this. I talked openly with all my children about
this issue and they knew full well how to prevent it yet, here we were. We sat on the
floor in the hallway and talked and cried and I assured him that everything would
be ok. I loved him no matter what and we could get through anything together. After

all that we had made it through, this seemed like nothing. Monty's fear soon turned to excitement. Monty always wanted a baby. He began telling me so when he was about five years old. I remember him telling me that he didn't care if he had a wife, but he was sure he wanted a baby. But things didn't go as we hoped they would. Through tears he told me that at the first doctor appointment, the doctor said something was wrong with the baby and it did not seem to be growing correctly. Monty was scared. Within a couple of weeks, it was confirmed that she had lost the baby. Monty was devastated. There are so many things in this life that we wish to keep far from our children, and this was one of those things.

We all wish life only had happy times, but this is not reality. Around the time we were grieving the loss of Monty's baby, one morning as I was getting ready to start my day, I got a phone call. From the other end of the line I heard my oldest son say the words, "Garrett is dead." I struggled to process what I had just heard. This couldn't be right. Garrett, my nephew, was only 15 years old. How could this possibly be? People in my family don't die, especially 15-year-old kids. My family had been so blessed with only two deaths my entire life, one being my uncle who died of cancer and the other my grandfather, who died at the age of 84 in a fire. Children weren't supposed to die. This was the first time something of this tragic magnitude would touch our family, but it wouldn't be the last. My sister, Tonya, and her husband, Tim, had begun building a new home. That morning, Garrett their son, had been riding a four-wheeler with a friend on the property where they had just broken ground. There were ruts everywhere from the heavy machinery that been excavating the ground where the house was to be built. As they rode along, the front wheel of Garrett's four-wheeler, sunk deep down into one of those ruts causing the ATV to flip end over end. He died instantly and his teenage friend had driven frantically back to their old house to get help. My boys, Monty and Chad, were there with Austin, Garrett's older brother, and they were on the scene prior to the emergency vehicles. Monty told me of Austin crying over the body of his brother, screaming out for God to please not take Garrett. He cried, "Garrett is the good son, you should take me not him." But that's not really the way God works. Garrett was a strong, Christian young man and he was ready. I think sometimes, those who are not ready remain on this earth longer because God is not willing that any should perish but that all should come to repentance, so He keeps giving them more chances. My sister reported that as she stood over her son's lifeless body, she heard the most beautiful singing. She described it as angelic. She looked all around and asked where that singing was coming from but no one else could hear it. She believed that the sound she was hearing, was the angels singing as they welcomed her son into heaven. Garrett's death was a wakeup call for me. I had always believed in God but was living as if I had all the time in the world to get back to Him. I always planned to do it…someday. When Garrett died, it was apparent that we don't know if we have tomorrow, so I reasoned I needed to get it together now. I needed to be about getting my life together and serving God. No one is promised tomorrow. For the first time in my life I found myself taking on the sisterly protector role. I began calling her daily and stopping by often just to check on her. My older sister had always had that role but now she seemed so helpless and vulnerable. I watched her at the funeral and felt anger welling up inside of me. This whole funeral ritual that we do seemed to be nothing more than a cruel practice. Why do we do this anyway? I watched the shell of a person who used to be my sister with the perfect life, listen to person after person acting as if they "understood" what she was going through. How was she so strong? How was she handling this with such grace? If this were me, I couldn't do it. They don't know how she feels. I was angry at the well-wishers saying things like, "He is in a better place." Her child was dead. How is that helpful? My heart ached for her. How does one ever cope with losing their child?

This was the beginning of a more intentional walk with God for me. I began praying more and seeking God's will for my life in a way I never had before. I had begun attending a mega church and I walked out of church one Sunday morning bursting with excitement. Our church had revealed that, due to an abundance of giving, they had more than they needed to make budget, so they were giving money back. Everyone walked forward to take an envelope from the offering plate with instructions to pray about the money they received. We were to then give it to someone and report back in three weeks on how God used the money. I immediately began imagining a poor hopeless mother, whose children had no coats to wear or food to eat. My envelope contained $20 and I diligently searched everywhere I went for someone in need. I prayed in earnest for God to send me just the right person and I was so enthusiastic, at first. After a week went by without one single candidate, I began to get a bit worried. I prayed harder and searched arduously but to no avail. As we entered the third and final week before we were to have completed our task, I became wholeheartedly stressed. This was not fun anymore. Why wasn't God showing me who was to receive this money? I had been praying, so why wasn't He answering?

Then it happened. One day while at work, I heard God's voice telling me to add $80 of my own money to the $20 I had received and give it to Christina. I quickly chastised myself. Christina had no children. She was a single woman and she had a job. This idea was simply ludicrous. I wondered why I would entertain such a foolish notion and I pushed it to the back of my consciousness. A short time later, I heard the voice again. Once more I dismissed the thought as absurd and reminded myself that not only did Christina not have any children, but also that I was a single mother of three who surely needed that $80 much more than she. Frustrated with my illogical mind, I pushed the thought away once again. After a few moments, I heard the voice for a third time. Exasperated, I told God that I had plans for this money and Christina was not what I had in mind. I intended to help a poor jobless mother but if this were what He truly wanted, then I would comply.

I hesitantly walked next door to Christina's office. She and I were friendly, but not really friends. She was basically just a coworker who I knew nothing about and the thought of handing her $100 was a bit unnerving. What if she were offended? I took a deep breath and knocked on her door. As she invited me in, I quickly blurted out, "Christina, I have no idea why, but God just told me to give you $100." As tears welled up in her eyes, she stood silently staring at me. My mind raced as I tried to find the words to repair the offense I had just rendered to this poor unfortunate victim of my insanity. She then began to speak and through her tears, told me that she was struggling with whether or not God was real. As she grappled with these thoughts that morning, she had decided to pray about it. A few minutes before I had knocked on her door, she had prayed, "God, if you are real, please show me." She then revealed that even though that day was payday, she had found herself $100 short on her rent. Through tears and hugs I was able to share Jesus in a much larger way than I had ever dared to dream of. I had big plans for that money, but God's plans were even bigger. As I walked away, I thought of how I had almost talked myself out of being part of God's perfect plan and marveled at both His patience with me, and His precise timing. Because I was willing to listen to God's voice, even when it seemed illogical to do so, He was able to show Himself to someone at the exact time they needed to see Him. God's plan and timing are perfect and if we will let Him use us, we may just be blessed beyond our wildest imagination as God reveals Himself to us in the most improbable ways. I wondered if all those times, I thought God hadn't heard me or at the very least hadn't done anything, I was wrong. Maybe He had been there all along but just had a bigger plan than my own. Maybe He had kept His plan hidden because it was bigger than I could even think of.

"My thoughts are nothing like your thoughts," says the LORD. "And my ways are far beyond anything you could imagine." Isaiah 55:8 NLT

Later that week when I went to pay my car payment at the bank, I tore two payment coupons out because the first was a bit past due so I figured I should just go ahead and pay two. The teller looked quizzically at me and informed me that those two payments were not past due, they had already been paid. I informed her that there must be a mistake. I still had the coupons and I would not have made a payment without using them. She stood there shaking her head, checking her computer and verifying that it was not a mistake. Those two car payments had been paid in full, but I knew it was not by me. I never knew who paid those two payments, but I knew that somehow, some way, God had made sure they were paid in response to me listening to His voice. He had paid me back exponentially by covering those two payments.

Financially, things seemed to be going well and I loved my work. After multiple promotions, my boss now was the corporate therapy director and he was amazing to work for. He promoted me regularly and gave me a raise every time I was offered another job. He said he didn't want to lose me. Eventually, he decided that we needed to meet once or twice a month in Indy to discuss therapy. He was a handsome man and so successful. Our meetings were filled with talk of his success rather than discussion of my work, but I didn't mind. He always paid me for the full day of work and bought my lunch. Besides, he was dreamy! I hardly heard anything he said as I stared into his gorgeous eyes and wished he felt the same as I did. Then one day it happened. He asked me to meet him in a nearby town to talk. The meeting place was the parking lot of a hotel, which didn't even register with me. Once I arrived, he told me of his secret feelings for me and kissed me passionately. My head was swirling. This amazing man was interested in me. Maybe I had finally found the man of my dreams. I looked forward to pursuing this relationship and really getting to know him. I fantasized about him taking me out on the town, introducing me to all his friends. Finally, I thought, I had found a quality man. We talked daily on the phone with conversation heavily laden with flirtatious innuendoes until the day he showed his true colors. He came right out and asked me to meet him back at the same hotel. I naively asked him to explain exactly what he was asking me for.

He said he wanted to have sex. I was shocked, hurt and disappointed. Fighting back tears of disappointment, I firmly told him that was not the type of relationship I was looking for. He tried frantically to back track and explain his misstep by telling me I didn't understand how long he had been denying his needs because he was my boss and it was forbidden. I told him that I could appreciate that, but I still held firm that I was not interested in that type of relationship. After that, I never was invited to lunch, or to a motel by him again and I was fine with that. I began to doubt myself and my ability to choose a man of quality. I was, however, very thankful that he took my pay rate to the top of the pay scale before finding out that I was a dead end. He didn't dare retract it, for fear of a sexual harassment lawsuit. Years later, he was in all the papers being led off to jail. It became clear that his relationship with me was not the only thing sketchy he was involved with. He was arrested and jailed for stealing from the company he was leading. God was definitely protecting me from that one.

Back at home, things seemed to be going pretty well. Monty, my oldest, was a senior in high school and Chad was a junior. It was fun watching them over the past 3 years play on the high school basketball team together. Senior night was coming and, much to my dismay, their father announced his plan to come. I had so many emotions about this. I was excited that it would be Monty's senior night. He had made it all the way through high school and would be honored for all his accomplishments. On the other end of the spectrum, his abuser intended to show up to claim some sort of glory for who this boy had grown to be. I was irritated that he would walk out on that gym floor with me and my son and act proud of him. He had no right to that honor. All he had ever done was hurt him, but somehow Monty, kept allowing him back. He so wanted him to be his dad, to be proud of him. I knew I could not forbid this from happening, but I could ensure everyone would see him for the little man he was by wearing the highest heels I could find. There was also a very small amount of fear still lingering. I still had those horrid nightmares.

The evening of the big game, Monty was filled with excitement. He was built for basketball. He had grown to be a staggering 6 foot 5 inches and weighed 220 lbs. He was always a force to be reckoned with but on this night, he played out of his mind. When it was all said and done, Monty finished the game with 48 points and 20 rebounds. As usual, I rushed down to the floor to congratulate him after the game, but his father had beat me to him. I got there in time to see Brandon tell his son, good game and goodbye. Then he was gone. Monty stood there in heartbroken disbelief. He looked at me with tears in his eyes and said, "Mom, everything I did tonight was for him, every steal, every point, every rebound. I thought if I did enough to make him proud, he would want to stay. But it wasn't enough." Monty quickly wiped the tears from his eyes and outwardly moved on. He went back to the happy-go-lucky Monty that everyone loved, and no one knew how much he was hurting on the inside.

Monty Ervin pours in 48 as Rockets hold off Southern

BY DANIEL HARRIS
News-Gazette Sports Writer

Rick Reed photo

Union's Monty Ervin posed a big problem for visiting Randolph Southern Friday night at the Launching Pad as the senior scorched the nets for 48 points, tying a school record held by Danny Farmer. Ervin's hot hand helped the Rockets overcome an 18-point deficit in the first half to rally past the Rebels for a thrilling 89-86 victory on "Senior Night."

MODOC – You can call it only a game, but when it is played like it was Friday night between the Union Rockets and the Randolph Southern Rebels, it is something special.

The Union Rockets erased an 18-point first half deficit, and behind a school-record tying 48 points from Monty Ervin, they claimed an 89-86 win.

On the Rockets' "Senior Night", it was the Rebels coming out early and setting the tone. Steve Warren's back-to-back threes gave Southern an early 16-4 advantage.

"Our kids really came out to play tonight. And if we can put two halves together like we did in the first half tonight, good things can happen," said Southern coach Shane Osting.

Monty Ervin had yet to score a point when Rocket coach Aaron Groves called a time out after Warren's second three.

Ervin scored the final six points in the first quarter, and then scored all but one of his team's 15 points in the second quarter.

But behind a great team effort by the Rebels, the visitors stretched the lead to 18 at 41-23 with 2:05 remaining in the first half.

Union scored the last five points of the first half, and then exploded out of the gate in the third quarter.

Chad Ervin, who had only managed a single point in the first half, scored 12 points in a three-minute span. And when Chad was not scoring, his brother was. Monty added another 10 in the third quarter, and Union trailed by just one after three periods of play.

Monty added another 18 points in the final quarter and actually had a chance to set a new school record and break the existing county record of 49 points, but he missed a pair of free throws with 15 seconds left.

While Monty was tearing up the record books, Allen was showing why he is also one of the best players in the county. He scored 15 of his team-high 37 points in the final quarter. He had a chance to tie the game, but his three went wide left as time ran out.

Allen's 16 made free throws was just one shy of the Rebels' school record.

"Wow, wow, wow! What a game of runs," a thrilled Rockets coach Groves said after the game. "They had a great first half run, we had a great third quarter run, we got up by 10 and they made anoth-

cr run. But we held on despite some stupid mistakes," added Groves.

When the game was on the line, the Rockets went inside time and time again. And the Rebels just could not slow them down.

The win had another special impact for the Rockets.

"There are two kids that made a huge difference for us tonight," Groves said. "Obviously Monty with 48 points and 21 rebounds. And the other kid was Andrew Craw – not only by the way they played, but they both told me to start Dane Wisener (a fellow senior) in place of them because they love Dane as a teammate. As a coach that does my heart good."

Wisener not only started the game Friday night, he also hit the team's first field goal.

The Rebels, who end their regular season 2-17 and 1-6 in the

league, also got 21 points from Warren. Brock Mills put up 10 in the loss.

The Rebels play Blue River in the first round of the sectional Tuesday night.

Chad Ervin was the only other Rocket in double figures as he hit for 16. Monty Ervin's 20 field goals was a school record, and he came just two rebounds shy of that record.

The Rockets improve to 5-14 and 3-4 in the MEC. They will play Union City in the bye game next Friday in sectional action.

The junior varsity game was not nearly as thrilling, but there were still a lot of great efforts. Steven Lanier had his best game of the season on the second team as he led all scorers with 22 points as the Rockets prevailed 50-32. Garrett Swaim added 12 points in the win.

Game summary

Southern	22	41	58	86
Union	12	27	55	89

REBELS – Mills 3 4-10 5 10; Warren 3 1 9-10 2 21; Deatline 2 0-0 4 4; Pruitt 1 2 0-0 2 7; Allen 5 3 16-20 4 37; Stevenson 2 1-2 1 5; Baker 1 0-0 0 2; Hutzell 0 1-2 4 1. Totals 14 31-44 23 86.

ROCKETS – Wisener 1 0-0 1 2; Davis 3 1-2 4 7; Wiles 0 2-4 0 2; M.Ervin 20 8-12 3 48; Swaim 1 1 0-0 5 5; Craw 0 0-2 2 0; C.Ervin 2 4 2-4 5 16; Morehous 1 3-4 3 5; Patterson 2 0-0 3 4. Totals 3 32 16-30 26 89.

Junior Varsity

Southern	10	14	20	32
Union	12	19	40	50

REBELS – Baker 2 1-2 5 5; D.Woftal 0 0-0 2 0; Austin 2 1-2 4 5; C.Woftal 1 2-6 5 4; Pegg 1 1 0-0 0 5; Welling 1 1-1 2 3; McNutt 1 0-0 1 2; Bleill 0 0-0 2 0; Anguiano 0 0-0 0 0; Bragg 1 0-1 1 2; Morrison 2 0 0-2 1 6. Totals 3 9 5-14 23 32.

ROCKETS – Lanter 1 6 7-10 2 22; Pitman 0 0-0 3 0; Moore 0 1-2 2 1; Swaim 4 4-9 2 12; Beaty 2 0-0 2 6; Brown 1 2-2 5 4; Patterson 1 3-8 1 5. Totals 3 12 17-31 17 50.

Newspaper write up for Monty's big senior night game.

149

Monty went on to graduate from high school and was asked to play basketball at a small college in Iowa. It was so exciting, and I had a sense that Monty had made it. He had graduated high school and was now starting the adventure of the next part of his life. My excitement soon turned to worry as things started unraveling. He had left the love of his life back home in Indiana and they missed each other terribly. Then there was the coach. He not only yelled at the kids, he demeaned them. This was bringing back many horrific memories of his childhood and Monty struggled to tolerate it. Monty had always been tough and was determined to overcome this challenge as well. But a college basketball career would not be in the cards for Monty as one day, before playing his first college basketball game, he fell from the top of a bus he was cleaning for the coach and injured his back. He was prescribed prescription pain pills to get through the pain but was eventually deemed unable to play. He returned home soon after. He didn't act like it bothered him. He seemed happy to be home and back with his girlfriend. He immediately went to work and found a small house to rent. The first time I went to visit him in his new home I was quite surprised to hear him ranting and raving about half-empty pop cans and lights being left on and trash scattered around the living room. He had friends over the night before and they apparently were not yet living on their own and had left things in disarray. Monty was saying things like, "They don't pay for the groceries or the light bill" and "Why can't they pick up after themselves?" All this time, I thought he wasn't listening but apparently, he was. Maybe my motherly advice hadn't fallen on deaf ears. Even with dropping out of college, Monty seemed to be happy with his life. He had plans to become an electrician and was as happy as I had ever seen him.

I, however, was not so happy. My love life was in the toilet. I determined I must surely, but sadly, be destined to be alone. At least I had my children. If not for them, I don't know what I would have done. That year on my birthday, I set my phone ringer to play the happy birthday song every time it rang but it never rang all day. No one called, only emphasizing to me more that I was alone and had no one to care. Feeling worthless as I arrived home that evening, I walked into my house having my own private birthday pity party. Once inside I found the most beautiful bouquet of flowers on my dining room table. I quickly ran to grab the card to see who had remembered. The card read, "Happy Birthday to the most beautiful girl in the world. It's good to be your son!" Chad had saved the day. He had remembered. I could always count on him.

12

NEW HOPE

had become totally disillusioned by my dating experiences. I became very bold in stating my expectations prior to each date. I was not interested in sex. Each suiter initially agreed but their true colors would emerge by the end of the night, signaling to me that there was not going to be a second date. I tired of the meaningless banter, of the nighttime chats with random men and lost all faith in the dating websites. I had discovered that putting my true income only attracted men who wanted to be taken care of. I changed my profile to look like I made less but demanded more income from any prospective suiter. I was frantically trying to control the situation but was obviously failing miserably. At this time of my life, I was completing one hour of cardio every morning and had many different paths outside I would rotate between to get this done. One beautiful morning I was walking along a nature trail and praying to God, telling Him all my struggles and fears and finally, in desperation, threw my hands out and said, "Take it God. I don't want it. I am giving it to You. If You want me to find someone to live my life with, then You do it. I obviously do not know what I am doing." I was so over it. I had discontinued using every website but one and I don't know why I even kept that one open. Every potential match they sent to me I would immediately delete. I just didn't believe it was ever going to happen. I even quickly deleted the match with the name Chip Mehaffey when his picture appeared on my profile. I glanced at his picture and yeah, he looked good, but so did a lot of others and they always end the same. What I didn't know is that when they sent me his profile, they also sent him mine and he saw something that interested him. It wasn't my picture. For some reason, my picture wasn't showing up for him. What interested him was what I said in my profile. I said I wanted someone who loved me like my Grandpa loved my Grandma. He would later tell me that usually if someone didn't have a profile picture, they didn't get a second look but, for some reason, he decided to read my profile.

Chip emailed me July 31, 2005. I recognized the name, as one I had recently show up on my page. We sent several more emails back and forth to try to get a feel for each other and it didn't take long to figure out that we were closer in proximity to one another than either of us had thought. In an attempt to protect his privacy, Chip had listed his home as Muncie, but eventually admitted that he lived in Winchester. I was taken aback because that is the town where I worked. I was there every day and may have easily run into him unexpectedly. This connection was becoming a lot less safe. He also told me he coached basketball at the local high school. A high school that my boys played against. I asked my boys if they knew the coach of Winchester boys' basketball, and after some amusing antics mimicking this apparently successful and well-known coach, they asked to look at his picture to see if he were smiling. It seemed, he had a reputation for being intense and was not often seen smiling. He did know my boys and he knew them by name. After finding out where I lived growing up, he reported that he used to go to that town to get ice cream. Chip didn't know it at the time, but that ice cream shop was next door to where I grew up. After telling him where I went to school, he told me about a friend of his from church camp and she was one of my best friends in high school. We could remember a time after a ballgame being introduced but neither had been interested at that time. We had other more important things to attend to. We also mused that we had both attended several games our junior year at New Castle to watch Steve Alford play. Well, he may have gone to watch the game, but I went to make the rounds around the top of the gym to socialize. None the less, we had so many chances to have met years ago that it seemed less than coincidental. That safe anonymity was gone but somehow that made this connection all the more exciting. We bantered back and forth through email and I looked forward to hearing from him. We were already making each other laugh. By August 3rd he had sent me his phone number and it was on. He soon asked me to meet. I was nervous but excited. I usually would be thinking, "This is a big waste of my time, I know I am not going to like this guy. I have so many other things I could be doing." But for some reason, this felt different. I cared what this guy thought of me. I wondered what was wrong with me and reminded myself I could not lose my edge. I had to stay in control. Then I remembered that I had given this to God. Why did I have so much trouble leaving it there? Why did I feel such a strong need to control it? I think it was likely due to feeling as though I had very little control during any of the first 38 years of my life that now that I had a tiny bit of perceived control, it was difficult to relinquish.

The day of our first date was finally set and the nervousness began to set in. It was one thing to joke and talk big over some dating site, but it was quite another to be meeting in person. In reality, I am painfully shy. That old familiar feeling of not measuring up began to set in. You can totally control what a person sees of you when you are only presenting what you choose to present online. When you meet someone in person, they really see you and I wasn't sure he would like who I really was once he knew. I set about ensuring I would make a good first impression, choosing the perfect outfit and making up my face and hair. All these things were things I could control. When he showed up at my door, I liked what I saw. He had a gorgeous smile and seemed laid back and easy going. I loved the confidence he exuded. It was an "I don't even have to try" type of confidence. He knew who he was and what he had to offer. So far, so good. As I gracefully walked to his car and got in, I looked like I too had it all together, but I was screaming inside. I was so nervous. What was this about? I had given up on finding the right guy. I had given up on caring. They were all the same anyway right? They were all lacking, and I knew I would eventually have to simply settle. It wasn't a matter of finding the perfect guy, it had become a matter of what I could tolerate. Why did I begin to care now? He tried valiantly to make small talk along the way, but he was met with short one-word answers. This was the me I didn't like. The me that freezes up with fear. I silently chided myself but try as I might, I couldn't make myself be that outgoing, fun loving person I wished I was. He likely felt like I did when meeting the imposter lock jaw date with someone else's picture. He probably was thinking, your voice sounds like the same person, but what happened to your personality?

He had picked the most perfectly picturesque setting for our first date. It was a restaurant on a lake, called Ainsley's Café. We sat outside, overlooking the water. The scenery was breathtaking. As I took in the beauty of God's creation and felt the soft breeze blowing through my hair I began to relax. I looked at this man and wanted to know who he was. I became totally engaged in the conversation and we both became so enthralled that the waitress felt the need to apologize for interrupting to take our drink order. We swiftly obliged her and went right back to our conversation. I understand the need for speed when your income depends on turning tables quickly, yet I couldn't seem to think of anything other than the man sitting in front of me. The poor girl had to return four or five times before we could remember to look at the menu to make a choice on dinner. It was kind of embarrassing yet also invigorating to find such an interesting man that could make the rest of the world seem irrelevant. We spent much more time talking than eating and it felt as if we were the only two people on the planet. Things with him were easy, comfortable somehow. I remember being snapped back to reality by the man's voice coming from the table next to us. He was saying something about being sorry that his party was so loud when it was obvious that we were wanting a quiet dinner. I smiled coyly thinking, "I didn't even see your family of eight sitting right next to us, let alone hear you being disruptive" but simply said, "You were no bother." We finally finished and thought it best to free up the table for this kind server whose source of income we had held captive for entirely too long. I made a mental note of his generous tip and we headed to the car. Neither of us were ready for the evening to be over so we went to a park near my home, where the intimate conversation continued as we walked down the winding path. I was unaware of time passing as we talked the night away as though we were old friends. The conversation only stopped for a moment when he decided to steal that first kiss. I felt as though I would be carried away by the butterflies dancing inside my chest. What was happening here? I knew I must get ahold of myself. I was letting this man carry me away, which my experiences had taught me was a dangerous situation, but I just didn't care. I wanted him to carry me away. I wanted him to be real. We reluctantly agreed, it would be best for him to take me back to my house. It was getting late and we both needed to get some rest. On the ride back to my place I wondered if he too would fail this one last test of the night. I had made it clear to him that I was not interested in a physical relationship until marriage and he of course agreed wholeheartedly. I say "of course" because they all said they agreed, but in the end, it was always the same; a huge disappointment when they hadn't meant what they said, resulting in me blocking their number from my phone. Would this be another one of those? Did I dare hope? The chemistry between us was undeniable and instantaneous. Once he walked me to the door of my home, it took us another three hours to say goodnight, but he never tried anything. He was true to his word. Who was this man and what was he doing to me?

We were both trying our best to take things slowly. He had been hurt before as had I. But try as we might to rein this thing in, we were riding full speed ahead. For two weeks we talked nearly every day on the phone and even met mid-week for lunch. The first time he held my hand and prayed aloud, it took my breath away. I thought I must be living in a dream. Did this man have any flaws? He had warned me that he didn't just introduce everyone he dated to his daughter, so I didn't take it lightly when he informed me that he thought it was time. We planned it out for me to be at his house when she arrived home from school. I was anxiously awaiting her arrival, but when she walked through the door it was instantly apparent that she did not share my enthusiasm. She was polite enough, but quickly retreated into her bedroom quietly closing her door behind her. I thought maybe she just needed time to get used to the idea of sharing her daddy with someone and hoped it would be better the next time we met up. The next day, I was there when she returned home from school and apparently, she thought we hadn't understood her position on the matter and needed to make it more clear to the both of us. On this day she walked through the door, glared disapprovingly at me, stormed down the hallway to her room and defiantly slammed her door. Chip glanced at me apologetically and proceeded down the hall for an impromptu lesson on how we treat our guests. He informed her that she would not be staying in her room this afternoon and that she was to choose a game for us all to play. She obeyed, well sort of. She brought out the two-person game of Battleship in one last ditch effort to reclaim her daddy from this new woman who was threatening their relationship.

I drove home that evening consumed with worry. I knew him well enough to know that Mackenzie was his world and that if she didn't want me around, I would not be around for long. I prayed for God to work things out and it wasn't long before she warmed up to me. The day I knew we had turned a corner we had gone to a local street fair. Mackenzie wanted to ride the Wipe Out Ride, but her dad pretended he did not want to. I eagerly agreed to go, and we rode it over and over again, laughing the whole while. After the evening was over and we headed back to the car, 8-year-old Mackenzie, reached out and took my hand. I was silently cheering inside. I had finally won her over.

Just because Mackenzie was willing to open her heart to me did not mean her daddy was willing to. We were both dating other people but, to be honest, I didn't want to. He is the one I thought of as soon as I opened my eyes every morning. He was the one on my mind as I drifted off to sleep every night and he was the one who crept into my thoughts all day long. He thought it amusing to talk about the other woman he was dating who had the same name as I, referring to her as Stacy #1, and me as Stacy #2, due to the fact that he met her first. I was not amused! I was never satisfied with second place. I was playing it cool on the outside, never calling him more than once before he called me and only answering every other one of his calls. I knew the game and I knew how to play it well. I understood that men need to be the pursuer rather than the pursued, but inside I didn't want to play games. I wanted to be able to just be me and have that be enough. But there were games to be played and we were both veteran players. I quickly noticed that along with each new date, came a new challenge. He appeared to be attempting to test me to see if I were a worthy partner. I had passed the initial test of being accepted by his daughter, but the tests were only beginning. I passed his family test after being accepted by his parents and siblings. I passed his intelligence test after teaming with him to beat his sister and her husband in Euchre. I passed his intestinal fortitude test by being able to withstand playing tennis for hours in 100-degree weather with the sun beating down on us. I passed his athleticism test by being a sport while learning to play golf, a game I had never played before. I passed his idiot test by refusing to hold his disgusting maggot infested trash can so he could safely stand 5 feet away and spray it out with a hose. But there was one test that would prove harder to pass and that was the test of truly being a follower of Jesus. He had been fooled in his past dating experiences and was not about to make that mistake again. That could only be proven by many long talks about faith and many months of living out my faith for him to see.

After finally passing all his tests, something changed. I had stopped over at his house for our usual mid-week lunch date and he wasn't acting like himself. He was distant. I finally asked him what was going on and he told me he needed space. I don't know what else he said because once I heard those words, I was no longer listening. My mind was racing as I tried to figure this out. I quickly closed my heart and abruptly left. What a fool I had been. I knew better than to trust this man. He had warned me one day that he didn't do needy, so if I wanted to stay in the picture, I wouldn't act that way. Had I been too needy? I didn't think so. I was pretty independent and made sure to not smother him. I knew better than to put myself in a position where someone would have the power to hurt me. For eight years, I had been smart. Never letting anyone get close enough to hurt me so why now had I let my guard down. I was an idiot. He would never do this to me again. I cried all the way home. Once I got home, I proceeded to reinstate my online dating profile. I was moving on. Almost instantaneously I had returned to that cold, unfeeling person I had discovered myself to be on that day eight years ago when emotionlessly holding my crying daughter. What a hold our past can have on us. That evening as I lay in bed, I grabbed my most recent choice in self-help books and opened to the place I had left off. I read when a man finds himself falling in love, it is scary. Before a man can commit his life to someone, he must first be sure that if she were gone, he would miss her. Wait, what? I read it again. Could that be what was going on? Could his request for space mean he is falling in love with me? And did God just put this page in front of me at the perfect time, just when I needed to see it? A little gleam of hope was creeping back into my heart. I tried to resist it, but it was too late, hope had returned. I had told God that this journey of my life was His to do with what He wanted so as scary as this was, I had to trust Him. That didn't mean, however, that Chip was off the hook. He needed to miss me, huh? I certainly knew how to make that happen. I quickly busied myself. I reached out to old girlfriends that I hadn't seen in a while and made plans to ensure I would be busy whenever he decided he missed me. I watched my phone impatiently for his call with a resolution that I most definitely would not be available when it rang. After what seemed like an eternity, my heart leapt as his number appeared on my phone as an incoming call. I resisted the urge to pick up and hear his voice, but I knew what I must do. After a couple of days and a couple more missed calls, I picked up. He wanted to forget what he had said. He didn't want space, he wanted me. I was thanking God for showing me what was really going on before I closed off my heart for good.

While I was going through this time of testing, my oldest son Monty had gotten engaged to be married to his high school sweetheart. I was more than excited. Danielle was a beautiful and charming girl who would make the perfect partner for my son and daughter-in-law for me. Once again however, Monty wanted to invite his father. A child never seems to lose that longing to be loved and accepted by his father. This meant I had to come face to face with this man once again and I had to do it alone. Chip and I were not far enough along in our relationship for him to come to the wedding with me. We had only been dating for a month and a half, so I had to face him all by myself. I put on a good face and no one knew the fear and disappointment I felt on the inside. The nightmares came back full force and I longed for peace. How long would I be tormented by this man? I was angry that he still had any semblance of control over me. At times I wondered if he were dead, would I be free? As quick as this thought would enter my head, I would be filled with shame. How could I think that way? I was supposed to forgive. I couldn't seem to do that. Here I was wishing him dead. The bible says in Mark 11:25 that we must forgive others so that God can forgive us. I reasoned that until I could forgive my ex-husband, God must not have forgiven me and since I sometimes wished him dead, I surely had been unable to forgive him. I could not figure out how to get past this. Most of the time I did not wish bad for him, but I certainly didn't feel love for him or want any kind of relationship with him. Just the thought of him brought nightmares. Why would I want that? I knew I did a lot of things right but in the forgiveness area, I was a failure and, try as I might, I didn't know how to fix it.

My relationship with Chip was growing stronger. We seemed perfect for each other. We just seemed to click. We laughed often and were settling into this seem-ingly perfect relationship when Chip dropped another bombshell. He told me that an old flame had contacted him that week. He wondered if God was trying to tell him he wasn't supposed to be with me. As I thought about it, I remembered an old flame reaching out to me that week as well. I simply told him to consider the possi-bility that not all opportunities come from God. I told him to consider the fact that if we are about to complete what God had destined for us and we were about to be-come a force to be reckoned with for God, do you not think that the devil would be doing everything he could to prevent that from happening? We both contemplated that possibility and our relationship only grew stronger.

Me and Chip four months into our dating relationship

After a slightly rocky start, Mackenzie and I bonded seamlessly. I played on the floor of the living room after school with her for hours and we became co-conspirators in a never-ending battle against her dad. We were always doing silly things to trick him, and he would playfully protest that we were ganging up on him. Beyond that phony offended exterior I could always see a look of underlying approval. It was a look that I often saw in my own father. Bonus points were given for reminding me of my dad. Chip was always a good sport, even eating grass flavored "Jelly Belly's" pretending to not know we were up to something and then delightfully spewing them out upon being told their flavor. Chip was an extremely protective father and had to be coaxed out of his comfort zone on many occasions. One afternoon as the three of us walked alongside a small pond, Mackenzie inquisitively asked if the water was warm or cold. As her father was saying we were not going to be finding out, I was saying "I don't know, let's find out." The two of us gleefully ran down and promptly stuck our hands in the murky pond water. This was a new way of life for Mackenzie. Sometimes I won, like the time I taught her to ride her bike without training wheels. I explained that at eight years of age, it was time and positioned Chip at the bottom of the inclined driveway while Mackenzie and I started up at the top. I assured her I had her as she started peddling toward her dad. I turned loose as her dad panicked and she proudly rode that bike all the way to him on the first try. Other times I was met with a firm "that's not happening", like when I encouraged her to jump from the swing when reaching the highest point. It was fun feeling the give and take that parenting should have. I had never felt that. My first experience in raising children was me having no voice in anything that happened. The second was me doing it all, with no one to bounce ideas off. Now I was finally feeling what it would feel like to share this role with another reasonable parent, and it was empowering. I began to find my place in this young girl's life. I truly felt as though I was adding something to raising her. I taught her how to play ball, completed crafty school projects with her and taught her that doing kind of scary things could be fun. I was amazed that she so quickly and completely accepted me.

When entering a relationship with someone who has been married before you are both going to have some baggage. There are going to be triggers for you that the other may not understand but, due to things that happened in the past, cause a certain reaction inside of you. We were learning to navigate these along with navigating the exes. This first hit us when, his ex-wife stopped by on her way home from work to drop off some of his dress shirts. I watched the exchange bewildered. Why did she have his dress shirts? He was oblivious to my thoughts but not for long. As soon as she was gone, I asked what that was about. He said that his shirts needed ironing. He hates ironing and she loves it so, he thought it would be fine to have her iron his shirts for him. Try as he might, he could not understand the problem with it. Finally, I explained it to him this way. Cars need oil changes. I don't like to change the oil in my car, but my ex is very good at it and actually enjoys doing it. I followed with, so would it be fine for me to contact him to ask him to change my oil then? He got the picture.

As we worked out the ground rules for our relationship, I had happily begun attending church with Chip. It was so nice to feel a bit like everyone else and have someone sitting by my side in the pew. Our church had started doing the study "40 Days of Purpose." I dove into the study with both feet. Since turning my life completely over to God on the path that day, I had been super excited to see what God would do next. I enjoyed reading the chapters and completing the assigned tasks until the day that spoke of being at odds with someone and making it right. My mind immediately went to my mother. I was angry with her for so many things but, mostly, I felt unloved by her. I felt as if I never measured up and would never be worthy of her love. I had intentionally distanced myself from her and found that I was happier if I didn't have to deal with her disapproval. But I didn't want to be at odds with anyone, certainly not my mother. I made the decision to attempt to set things right with her. I called her one morning and asked if I could come see her, then called to tell work I would be late. When I arrived at her house, I could tell she was a bit nervous as to what this was about. I had prayed the whole way there and was praying as I began to speak. I apologized for all the pain and disappointment I had brought into her life. I apologized for embarrassing her by getting pregnant. She weakly attempted to deny that she had felt those things, but I called her bluff and apologized again. When I finished speaking, she apologized for all the hurt she had caused me and acknowledged that she had not always done things the right way. It was the nicest visit we had ever had, ending in tears and hugs. This was a good step in the right direction. One honest conversation did not take away all the pain and scars from both of our pasts, but it did bring us closer as mother and daughter. It seemed that maybe I was figuring out my way with regard to the relationships in my life.

13

PERFECT PLANS

Chip and I continued our crazy fun courtship and after about six months, I found the words "I love you" constantly on the tip of my tongue. Maybe I am old fashioned or maybe I didn't want to scare him, but I refused to say it first. It was so hard to keep it to myself. There was no doubt I loved this man. I loved the way he looked at me like he had just found the most precious treasure. I loved the way he poked at me teasingly, making me laugh. I loved the way his eyes smiled right along with his mouth when we were together. Most of all I loved his relationship with God. He was a Christian and it showed in every aspect of his life. One evening, rather than going out, he had asked me to help him hook up his stereo system at his house. I was game. Everything was fun with him and besides, I had learned years ago how to fix things and had been told in high school that I had a very logical mind so this would be a piece of cake. We crawled around the floor that evening plugging this thing in here and that thing in there and by trial and error and a lot of laughs ended up with a fully functional stereo system. He reached out his hand to help me up from the floor and as I stood, he wrapped his arms around me and said the most beautiful three words in the human language. "I love you." My heart felt as if it would explode. I was caught off guard. I wasn't expecting that when we were working together on a project but nevertheless, there it was. As I gazed into his eyes I quietly whispered, "I love you too." I was amazed that somehow God had brought us together. Two people whose lives had brushed alongside the other multiple times over the years but had never connected. God had given us many opportunities beginning in high school but, time after time, free will had taken us in different directions. I have heard it said, "If it's not God's will you can't force it and if it is God's will you can't stop it." Had God kept putting us in circumstances where we would meet again until we finally got it? This man was perfect. If not perfect, at least perfect for me. My early dating resolve for this not to get physical was waning. We shared so much natural chemistry and now we were saying I love you. It had become so hard to stay true to our commitment but whenever I was weak, he was strong, and I loved him even more for it. In six months, I had learned that this man was for real.

In March of that year, Whitney came home excitedly talking about a trip to Florida. A few of her underage friends, were planning a spring break trip and she was determined to go. After many long talks and discussions back and forth we decided that she and I would take off on a girl's trip for Spring Break. Some women may be afraid of driving alone for 1000 miles and maybe we should have been, but we weren't. With our snacks in tow, we took off on our adventure. We laughed, talked, listened to music, and forged an even deeper connection between mother and daughter. That week we had no cares in the world. We hung out at the beach tanning, boogie boarding and climbing dangerously on rocks to get that just right picture. We were two independent young women, afraid of nothing and loving life. While sitting at a stop light one afternoon following an all-day trip to the beach, Whitney suddenly blurted out, "Chinese fire drill." I looked at her wide eyed and accepted the challenge. We both opened our respective doors and to the sound of car horns and cat calls, completed our trek sprinting the full circle around the car, jumping back into our seats just before the light turned back to green, laughing the entire time. Our girl's trip to Florida is a trip I will never forget.

Me and Whitney ready to take off for Florida

Unfortunately, our time in Florida had to come to an end but, after a week of beach bumming it, my 17-year-old daughter was not nearly as excited to assist in the long drive home as she was on the way there, and whenever asked to take over, she was simply too tired. I didn't really mind. My mind was swirling with all the fun adventures we had shared over the past week. I drove the 15-hour drive which ended up a bit longer than that by the time you add in the times we stopped for gas and bathroom breaks. I drove it straight through because I was young and because I hadn't seen Chip for a week. We pulled into town late afternoon and Chip and I made plans to go out that evening. We met at his house and headed into town. On the way I noticed a nagging pain beginning in my lower back and it was enough that I mentioned it. I assumed it was from the long ride home in the car, with as few rest breaks as humanly possible. It wasn't a terrible pain but was a nagging pain. We arrived at the restaurant and Chip hopped out and headed briskly toward the door of the restaurant. I opened my door and attempted to do the same but when I stood, an intense pain shot through my back that took my breath. I steadied myself by gripping the top of the door as he turned and looked quizzically at me and asked what I was doing. I told him I was coming and started toward the door. The

PERFECT PLANS

pain was not subsiding but as I contemplated returning to the car or continuing into the restaurant, I noticed a chair directly inside the door. If I could just make it to that chair, I could sit and be fine. But it did not quite go as I expected and when I sat down, that intense pain shot through my back again. I was unable to sit. Chip helped me back to the car and we found that the pain was tolerable if I laid my seat all the way down. He wanted to take me to the hospital, but as a single mother of three with no insurance, I had become accustomed to dealing with calamities on my own at home. I told him to just get me to his house and I would lay on the floor. In the past, if something were out of whack in my back a few minutes lying flat on a hard surface would eventually result in whatever was out of place returning to where it should be. Had I known what was to come I would have had him take me to my house, but I expected that after a few minutes I would be fine. He reluctantly agreed and took me back to his house. He helped me inside and I struggled to get to a position of lying on his living room floor. I quickly discovered I was unable to lay on my back without excruciating pain but was able to lay on my stomach, face down on the floor with some relief. I then asked Chip to call Whitney and have her bring some medicine I had at home from a past back injury following a car accident. She brought me pain pills and muscle relaxers and I thought with time, this would resolve. As the night wore on, it became evident this was not resolving. Chip finally warily agreed to go to bed, giving me my cell phone with instructions to call him if I needed anything. I didn't think that through before agreeing to it. At 2 a.m. I awoke to discover that I needed to use the restroom. I looked at my phone and remembered his words. There was no way I was going to call my boyfriend and have him take me to use the toilet. We had vowed to wait until we were married to become intimate and although it had been difficult at first, it seemed to get easier as we neared the finish line. Regardless, I did not want him to see me like that. I tried to get up to no avail. I thought if I could manage to crawl into the bathroom, I would be able to grit my teeth and pull myself up onto the toilet. I began slowly scooting myself along the floor. Four hours later when Chip emerged from his bedroom, he found me 3 feet closer to the bathroom than he had left me. He inquired as to what I thought I was doing. Through tears I explained my predicament. Without hesitation, he lifted me up off the floor and carried me into the bathroom. He could not let go of me without excruciating pain, so he helped pull my clothes down and when I was unable to sit, held me up while I used the restroom. I would have been humiliated but I was in too much pain to really care.

When that was finished, he insisted on taking me to the emergency room. Once there, he went in and had them bring a gurney out with which to take me into the ER. They did and then proceeded to give me pain medicine and to run every test they could think of, finding nothing wrong and doing absolutely nothing to relieve the pain. Chip became infuriated after overhearing two nurses discussing my case in the hallway and saying that I had to be faking and just drug seeking. He politely, or not so politely, told them I was not faking, and they eventually gave in and, after giving me a prescription, sent me home. I am not sure if Chip wanted out of the caregiver role or not, but he took me home to my house. My son Chad took over in being my caregiver. He had always been so loving and compassionate. He had my bedroom set up like I was a queen, even going so far as to buy a tv and mount it on my wall. He had to take care of me for the seven days it took me to be able to stand again. Once able to stand, it was another two weeks before I could sit without pain. Eventually the pain subsided, and I was able to get back to life. It would be several more years before I would get a diagnosis.

I have often compared raising children to the ocean waves. Sometimes the sea is so peaceful just kind of flowing along, then when you least expect it bam, a huge wave blindsides you sending you reeling. It is the ebb and flow of parenting and you just have to ride out the waves knowing that at some point in time, peace will return. This was definitely a calm time in parenting with Monty and Whitney, but Chad was producing one huge wave. It seemed to me he was rebelling against himself. He was acting nothing like that sweet perfectionistic responsible child I had known him to be. He was that child whose room was always neat and tidy with everything in its place. He would always do the right thing. He would begin studying for tests two weeks in advance but now it was the opposite. His personality had done a 180 and I didn't know who this man-child was anymore. He was struggling to grow up and I was struggling to live with him trying to grow up. He was 19 years old and still living at home. He had no real responsibilities. Life had become one big party which included a little bit of college, a little bit of work, and a lot of fun and games. I had told him that at this age he didn't have very many rules imposed upon him by me, but I insisted that he respect me and not bring his party into my home. He was unable to comply. He felt entitled to the portion of my income I had so freely given him since beginning my career, and that was a source of argument at one time ending with his assertion that I owed him, he hadn't asked to be born. As this turmoil escalated, my lease was up on my home and I had decided to move

Winchester. There were many factors included in this decision including being closer to work, closer to Chip and a decrease in monthly rent. As time grew closer to the move, things escalated with Chad until I told him, he would not be moving to Winchester with me. It hurts me to this day to think of the incredulous look on his face. He looked like I had abandoned him just like his father had. It hurt both of us to the core. I just did not know how else to nudge his life back on the right track.

When moving day came, I was filled with doubt, but a firm resolve that something must change. The definition of insanity according to Einstein, is doing the same thing over and over and expecting different results, and I had come to believe that the only way things were going to change for the good with my son was if I quit enabling his poor choices. Chad had asked me and my dad to help him move into what was to be his new home. As we pulled up to a house in a sketchy part of town, I was scared. It felt as if we were moving him into a crack house. It was so scary that I was afraid to leave my dad standing in the alley behind the house alone. We did what had to be done and as my father and I somberly walked back to the truck and left my son in that God forsaken place my dad looked at me and said, "I hope we know what we are doing baby." Inside I hoped that as well, with all my heart but resolutely replied, "I hope he figures it out real fast." He did figure it out. After about two weeks he moved out of that place and into a nice apartment in a nice part of town. It was looking like I made the right choice, but the guilt weighed on me like a ton of lead. It is so hard to make tough choices when it comes to your children, especially when you are alone in making those choices.

Whitney and I moved into a modest older home in Winchester. Being an older home, the closet space was virtually non-existent, so we made one of the bedrooms into a walk-in closet. It was fun living with just the two of us. We shared clothes and late-night talks and I marveled at how much I was beginning to like this "mini-me." If she were not my daughter, I would most definitely want to be her friend. We rarely disagreed but when we did, our arguments seemed to be centered around her choice in boys. I know everyone thinks their child is special but I wanted her to avoid the pain and heartache I had endured. I was doing everything I could to prevent her from making the same mistakes and she seemed determined to choose a guy who had less to offer than she deserved. She started dating a cute, tan rich college boy and, as a young inexperienced high school girl, she couldn't see what my wiser eyes could see. I became very concerned when he dropped out of school and moved back home with his mom. He quit his job and was no longer looking all that attractive in my eyes. One evening she even asked for my hard-earned money, so the two of them could go out on a date. She explained that he didn't have any money and it had been a long time since they had been out, and they really wanted to go out to eat. I told her that if she was determined to be with him, she would need to get used to eating peanut butter and jelly and I didn't want to take away her opportunity to learn what that would be like so, I would not be financing their dinner out. When I tried to talk to Whitney about my concerns, she quickly became defensive of him and would not listen to reason. He made her laugh and that was all that mattered to her. I tried to help her understand that it was not going to be all that funny when she was supporting him, and he was sitting on her couch eating Bonbons every day, but my warnings seemingly fell on deaf ears. Eventually, I came to realize that the more I pushed her to dump this boy who I felt had nothing to offer her, the more she seemed pulled toward him. I decided to take another approach. I sat down and once again told her my concerns about her being with someone who wasn't her equal but what I said next was what made all the difference. I told her that I believed in her. I knew she was smart and had good judgement. I told her because of this, if she decided he was the one for her then I would support her decision 100%. I then sat back and turned the whole thing over to God, never discussing it with her again.

That summer Chip, myself, Whitney and Mackenzie tried going on a couple of outings to theme parks and the like, but things seemed awkward. Everyone was polite but unfamiliar. The potential family didn't seem to be blending naturally. I wondered if we would ever be a family. I, in my limited wisdom, thought I needed to find a husband, a surrogate father for my children, but now my children were pretty much raised. Whitney was 17, Chad 19 and Monty 21, it was a little late to try to bring a man in to influence them. I didn't understand why it hadn't worked out the way I wanted but I know God sees the bigger picture. He knows exactly what we need and what we are going to need, and orchestrates the events of our lives to work things out for good to those who love Him.

My daughter Whitney was a senior that year and in September her dad decided to surprise her on her birthday and show up in Indiana. She visited with him briefly at a ballgame and then when at home, she asked me if she had to stay and visit him for the evening. She explained that he had demonstrated no desire to see her or talk to her for the past ten years and asked if she had to drop all of her plans to accommodate him on this date. She said that she had already made plans with her friends and would much rather see them than him. I told her it was totally up to her and that I understood where she was coming from. She worriedly asked if I would be ok when he came to the house if I were alone. I assured her that I would but inside I was a bit afraid. He and I had not been alone since that night when he had tried to end my life. I had struggled with PTSD for the past ten years including nightmares, panic attacks and imagining seeing him in various cars following behind mine. I had grown stronger and more confident but retrieved the Mace out of my purse just in case there was a problem. I began praying for God to protect me and met him at the door, confidently safe guarded by my God and my Mace. When he arrived at my house, he didn't seem to mind that Whitney had already left for the evening. This made me think coming to see her was just a ploy to get to me. We sat at the small drop side, 2-person table I had purchased for $100 when Whitney and I had made the move to Winchester. It was a little too close for comfort, but it was better than inviting him further into my home. As we sat there, he began making his case for why I should take him back. He said, nothing he had done was all that bad and I should just get over it. He attempted to make excuses for his poor behavior stating that he was in poor health with his diabetic issues and that was the cause for anything he had done inappropriately. He then finished with a statement of undying love for me. He asked me to give him another chance to see that he had changed and that he would leave his wife in an instant if I would say the word. I sat silently because my mother had taught me that if I had nothing good to say I should just keep quiet but inside I was thinking, "What exactly was 'not that bad,' the fact that you beat the crap out of my kids while I looked on leaving me to feel like a worthless excuse for a mother or the fact that you attempted to kill me through strangulation and our very own thirteen year old son had to stop you?" Or maybe you were thinking about the fact that you haven't helped out financially with the many expenses that have been incurred while raising our three children over the past ten years. So, to "just get over it" did not seem like a viable option to me. Then there was the poor health excuse. I work in the medical field and see lots of people in various states of poor health and although I will admit that many are a bit grouchy, I would never tolerate habitual abuse from them, nor would I tolerate an attempt on my life.

That excuse just didn't hold water with me. Then I looked at the statement "I have changed," which was followed up with the assertion that he would leave his wife in an instant for me. The first part was proven false by the abuse that Monty had seen while living with him in Florida for a short time, but even if that had changed over the last six years, he had just told me his marriage vows to his current wife meant nothing to him. That seemed like exactly the same man to me. I was jolted from my thoughts when he demanded, "Look into my eyes and tell me you don't feel anything." I looked into those eyes. Those eyes that I had once seen forever in. Those eyes that I had fallen so deeply in love with. Those same eyes that would turn pitch black in an instant, narrowing and filling with evil. I looked him straight in the eye and resolutely stated, "The only thing I feel when I look into your eyes is disgust!" I readied myself for the outburst of rage that was to come, tightly gripping my Mace under the table, but to my surprise it didn't come. He dejectedly stood up from the table, turned and without another word walked sullenly out of my house. I had done it. I had stood up to the man who once had ruled my every move and came out victorious. We both knew I was not the same woman he had known ten years before. I was now confident and strong and would no longer let anyone abuse me.

That fall, Chip's family had arranged for all of us to meet for a harvest celebration. We would go on a hayride, drink cider and play games. I was looking forward to the evening but not just because of hanging out with his family. I knew a secret. Chip's brother, Matt, planned on proposing to his girlfriend that evening. It was all so incredibly romantic, and I loved watching the two of them that night knowing what was to come later in the evening for them. I envied Janie. She was so lucky to be loved so much.

I had begun thinking about marriage but, for some reason, Chip had never suggested looking at rings. This frustrated me but it seemed too forward to suggest it myself. I tried lingering on the pages of magazines that displayed wedding rings or watching intently when commercials about getting engaged were shown but he wasn't taking the hint. As each proposal worthy occasion passed us by including Christmas, Valentine's Day and my birthday I began to wonder if it would ever happen. Maybe it wasn't as difficult for him as it was for me to tear myself away each evening when it was time for me to go home alone. I enjoyed his company so much I found it hard to leave him. Perhaps he wasn't feeling it. One late afternoon as I was driving back into town, I got a call from him. He explained that he was at the fieldhouse where he coached basketball and needed my help with something. He asked if I would stop by to help him. He was all business when I arrived, as I have found with him is often the case. When he is doing something, he is not about to be diverted by any sort of distraction, no matter how alluring. At first, I had found this quality offensive because if I did not have his attention at the time, I could not seem to gain it, but now I had come to admire his ability to maintain his focus on what needed to be done. I got a quick greeting and then it was immediately right to the task at hand. He was having trouble closing a window that was up high and wanted me to climb up to it while he supported me so I wouldn't fall. I carefully climbed up on a chair and then up on top of a tall file cabinet to get up high enough to where I could see what I was doing. When I looked at the windowsill, there was something that looked out of place over in the corner of the window. I picked it up to investigate and audibly gasped when I discovered it was a ring. I turned to look at him standing watching this unfold with a huge grin on his face. I quickly climbed down, and he asked me to marry him. With tears in my eyes, I said "yes", of course yes. I wondered how this man continued to catch me off guard, but I loved it. I loved the adventure he made my life.

Chip and I finally decided on a wedding date. We were to be married June 9, 2007. I would have been happy simply going to the courthouse, but Chip had bigger plans. He arranged for us to be married on a beach in Marco Island, Florida. I began planning for the event and the first item on the to do list was to find a dress. I wanted something elegant yet beachy. I recruited my sister to travel to Indy to go dress shopping. We searched all the fancy stores in the mall and eventually found just the right dress. It was ivory with beadwork and an asymmetrical chiffon overlay that fell halfway between my ankle and knee. Next, my sister asked if I was going to wear Spanx. I had never heard of such a thing. She took me to the intimate's section of Nordstrom's department store to show me these tiny modern-day miracle girdles. For those who do not know, these undergarments are boasted to shape, flatten and tone with a comfortable non-binding material that is guaranteed to create a smooth transition to skin that won't show through clothing. Well, I had never heard of such a thing, but we decided we must both try one on. We each grabbed one and headed into the highfalutin Nordstrom dressing room. The attendant looked us up and down as though we were entering a private country club as the help, but we were not deterred. We chose side by side dressing rooms and began the process of putting these miracle garments on. I call it a process by intention, there is nothing easy about donning Spanx. My first sign this may not be as easy as previously expected was when the fabric began clinging to my calf. I summoned every ounce of strength I had in my fingertips and was about to give it a heave ho when I heard my sister grunting as she was doing the same. At this time, a stifled giggle escaped my lips. I do not know why it is exponentially harder to keep quiet when you are in a situation where grace and class are expected but try as we might we could not keep quiet. Between the groans and giggles, the snorts, and the panting, I was sure the attendant thought we had smuggled a couple of pot-bellied pigs into the changing room. By the time we got our undergarments in place we were hot, sweaty, fatigued and intensely amused and then we had to figure out how to remove them. I decided against the Spanx as part of my wedding attire for fear it might detract from the long-awaited honeymoon festivities. Overall, the day was a great success. We found my dress and shoes, beaded ivory flip flops, as well as the perfect khaki linen pants and ivory linen dress shirt for Chip to wear.

Chip and I had to begin planning for our future together. We determined his house would not be big enough and decided to sell it and buy a home that would be ours. We began looking at homes and struggled to find what we wanted within the budget we had set for ourselves. We finally settled on a beautiful home on a golf course that we loved, but the asking price was just out of our self-imposed limit. After praying about it, we sent in our offer. The sellers did not like the offer. They told us they felt as though they had reasonably priced their home and were not real keen on lowering it. After discussing it, they agreed to ask God for a sign. They wanted a sign that they could be sure would be from God and so they chose a most unlikely sign that only He could provide. It was winter and they told God that if they were to accept our offer that they needed to see a robin. Later that day, as they were driving home from town, the snow was coming down in sheets. She was disinterested in her dreary surroundings so occupied her attention with a book she had with her. All at once her husband exclaimed, "Did you see that?" She hadn't seen anything. She was reading her book. He went on to say that he had seen God's sign. There had been a robin flying along right beside their car in the snowstorm. She argued that since she hadn't seen it, it didn't count, and that God would have to send another for her to believe it. With tears in her eyes, she told us that as they arrived home and pulled into the drive, there sat a robin on the snow in their front yard. They had gotten their sign, twice, and agreed to our offer price. It is an amazing feeling, when you are able to actually see God working in your life. He is always working behind

1e scenes but when He allows you a glimpse of what He is doing, it somehow gives ou validation that you are on the right track.

This was a hectic and exciting time in my life, and as if all that was happening vas not enough, I learned I was to be a grandma. I was allowed in the delivery oom when my first grandbaby, Maleigh, was born. I almost felt as though I saw omething I wasn't meant to see, but I was so thankful to have been given the op- ortunity. When the baby was born, they laid her on her mommy's tummy, and I vas surprised that she wasn't moving at all. I watched in awe as life slowly entered er body, and her little fingers began to move, then her arms. As life began to flow hroughout her tiny body, I marveled at the miracle of birth. I had never seen it rom this perspective before, and it was quite amazing. The moment he laid eyes n his baby girl; tears filled my son's eyes. He was immediately smitten. There s nothing like seeing a big old teddy bear of a man holding a tiny newborn baby. ince he was a little boy, Monty had always wanted a baby, and now his dream was oming true. A mother wants nothing more than to see her children happy, and this vas arguably the happiest I had ever seen, my son.

Back at home, Chip and I decided, the next step would be to sell his home. Us- ng a realtor would give us more exposure to buyers but would also take a chunk of ur selling price. We decided to try to sell it ourselves, and with God's help, headed o the local Walmart to buy a sign to post in the yard. As we drove through town, ve noticed the many homes that were sitting empty and began to worry that his 1ome would not sell. Most of these homes were being represented by realtors and hey weren't moving. What were we thinking? We decided we would give God one nonth and then we would contact a real estate agent to assist us. It turned out God lidn't need a month. He only needed two weeks and selling the house was behind is. We got a buyer who was willing to pay the full asking price from simply praying ind putting a sign in the yard.

Along with the buying and selling of homes, we had a wedding to plan. I made ny own invitations and ordered a cake online. I found a cake adorned with beauti- ul edible seashells. The company would deliver the cake and place it over a platter prinkled with brown sugar made to look like sand. It was beautiful. I naively saw 10 reason to pay a venue to marry when we could simply walk out onto the beach ind be married. With the help of the internet, I estimated the time of sunset and set the time for everyone to arrive at 6:30 p.m. Chip arranged the travel plans. He,

Mackenzie, Whitney and I were to fly down early enough to go to the local court-house to get a marriage license. We would be staying in a condo one of his friends had offered us to stay in as a wedding gift. Monty, his wife, and Chad would then drive my car down for us to have after the wedding and we would buy them all tick-ets to fly home. We invited our parents, our brothers and sisters, and our children and asked Chip's brother, Matt, to perform the ceremony.

This was an extremely busy time as we each had to separately pack up our homes in preparation for moving into our new home together as well as prepare our new home to be moved into. I elicited the help of Chip's mother and sister to paint and clean which ended up being a great bonding time with my new family. At the same time, I was attempting to pack up my things while downsizing to enable our two households to be combined into one. It was at this time I realized I had certain tendencies toward hoarding. I could only imagine it was from living life previously without, but logically, I knew I had no need for six hairbrushes and 100 hair ties. I found myself physically unable to throw anything away that wasn't broken or un-usable, so the local thrift store became a daily destination. I was able to feel good about helping others in need while getting rid of the excess I had accumulated once I finally had the means to do so. The furniture that would not be needed, went to my children which also made me happy. While packing up my bedroom, I came across my self-help books. All those books I had purchased when attempting to secure a father for my children and a partner for my life. As I flipped through the books and reminisced about those tough times a paper fell out of one of the books. I picked it up to find that list. That "must-have" list that I had given up on so long ago. Just for fun, I thought I would see how Chip measured up. One by one, I was able to check those boxes, every single one of them. This man I was about to marry was everything I had wanted, plus some I hadn't even imagined. God had answered my prayers above and beyond all I had asked.

When the four of us arrived in Florida we went straight to the condo. It had two bedrooms. Whitney and I would be in one room and Chip and Mackenzie in the other. We had only a few days to finalize all our plans. We drove around to all the local beaches and none seemed private enough to have a wedding ceremony. We also learned that most of the pretty beaches were owned by hotels which charged a fee to use for a wedding and required reservations way in advance. What had we done? We thought we were being smart in our planning, but it was looking like we would have no place to be married. Panic was beginning to set in when my parents arrived in town. We stopped by to see them and were struck by the beauty of their hotel, The Marco Beach Ocean Resort. It was a tropical paradise beyond anything I had ever seen. I naively asked the hotel manager if we could be married there and he agreed. We would have the most beautiful backdrop of tropical foliage, flowers, sand and sea and it would cost us nothing. We went about finalizing all the last-minute details. We had to obtain a marriage license, secure a restaurant for a dinner with family the night before and arrange for the cake to be delivered to my mom and dad's hotel room where our reception would be held.

Whitney asked me when I would pick up my wedding bouquet and my heart sank. I hadn't thought of that. I had not ordered flowers. We promptly drove to a local shopping center and inquired at a random flower shop and much to my delight, they arranged the most beautiful wedding bouquet full of ivory calla lilies and greenery that looked as if they were taken directly from a tropical rain forest. If Murphy's Law is everything that can go wrong will, I felt as though we were living the opposite, everything that could go wrong won't. It was as if God's blessings were on every last detail.

All seemed right with the world that day as we prepared for our wedding. The day I had hoped for and prayed for was here. I was filled with nervous excitement as we readied ourselves for the day. As I ironed Chip's shirt for the wedding, he walked up behind me and asked me what I was singing. I hadn't even noticed I was, but after having my attention brought to it, I realized I was singing Brad Paisley's song "She's Everything." The chorus says, "She's everything I ever wanted and everything I need. I talk about her, I go on and on and on, 'cause she's everything to me." That song represented exactly how I was feeling about my future husband and everything I believed he felt about me. He made me feel like a precious treasure he had been fortunate enough to find.

Finally, the time came to leave the condo and head for the beach. We walked out toward the car and Chip realized he had left his wedding shirt inside the condo. He hadn't wanted to wrinkle it so was waiting to put it on once we arrived. He turned to go back in and then realized he had also left his keys to the condo inside. We had no way to get in and retrieve his shirt. His stress level was through the roof as we tried to figure out how we would get back in. There was a maintenance crew for the condos, but we wondered if we could reach anyone after 5:00 p.m. on a

Saturday. As we feared, they had already left for the day, but one of the kind maintenance men agreed to travel the 20 minutes back from his home, to let us in. After retrieving the shirt, we would be 30 minutes late to our own wedding that I had so perfectly planned to end with the sun setting as our backdrop. I quietly pondered what negative effects being married in the dark may have on the romantic concept I had envisioned. With nothing else to do but press on we hurried toward the beach where our family had already gathered. All fears of a ruined day quickly faded away as we arrived to our perfectly unplanned venue, at our perfectly unplanned half hour delayed time and were married, surrounded by our closest family with a single ray of sun, shining directly down onto the Bible that Chip's brother Matt was reading from. We were pronounced husband and wife as we watched the sunset and surveyed the beautiful world God created while marveling at God's willingness to turn our desperately flawed plans into His incomparable perfect plan for us.

Chip and I immediately following our wedding ceremony.

Our newly blended family. Monty, Danielle, me, Chip, Mackenzie, Chad and Whitney

We were married surrounded by our family. My dad, my mother, me,
Chip, his mama and his dad.

Chip and I watching the sunset. The perfect evening even if...

EPILOGUE

I was just finishing up a long day of work at the assisted living facility where I now spent the majority of my days. I had always been drawn to the elderly with their kinder, wiser attitude toward life. This new focus for my therapy had been a much-needed change from the rule and regulation filled long-term care facilities that had previously been my primary source of work. The move to providing treatments at the assisted living facility could not have come at a more perfect time. I now got paid per visit and the pay was good. I was required to spend at least 38 minutes with each patient; however, I was able to spend as much time as I deemed appropriate. It was a welcome change. There was also no one pushing me to do group treatments or programs that were not appropriate. It was so nice to feel in control. As I arrived at Betty's apartment, I could feel myself relax just a bit. She was always so welcoming and happy to see me. I could really use a happy face right now. Once inside, she began with her usual chatter telling me of her struggles since seeing me two days before and excitedly worrying about her upcoming trip on a train to her granddaughter's wedding. She was so looking forward to going but ruminated on and on about her fears of not fitting into her dress on that glorious day even though there was not an ounce of fat on her tiny frame. Her big dilemma for the day, that she hoped I could help her solve, was what type of step stool she should buy to be able to climb on to turn the light on and off on her curio cabinet.

Betty was not only thin; she was also only about 4 foot 8 inches tall. After patiently explaining to her that a 92-year-old lady who uses a walker to ambulate probably should not be using any type of stool to climb on, we then went about problem solving a much safer solution for her quandary. In the end we ordered a switch that would go between the plug for the light and the outlet positioned waist high on the wall. I explained that we would leave the curio cabinet on all the time but now she would be able to turn the light on and off by simply flipping the new switch. As she hugged me and marveled at my "genius" mind, I was reminded why I loved her so much.

After making my way through a schedule of eight people with similar needs, I ended the day with an exercise group. It was always entertaining to watch these normally subdued elderly people come alive, dancing and moving to the music. Some days I used music from their teenage years, but on this day, I used modern pop music. It didn't seem to matter what music I chose, they relished in the attention and the activity, since both were scarce in the world they now lived. As was usually the case, there were smiles all around as we moved arms, hands, legs and feet to the beat of the music. When the session ended, they each lined up to get their weekly hug from their ever-willing therapist. I firmly believe one can never get too many hugs.

After dutifully completing all my paperwork and locking everything up, I began my long trek home. Since moving to Southern Indiana, I had been unable to find work close to home so was driving over an hour each way to the job site. I usually didn't mind the drive. It gave me time to decompress before arriving home and beginning dinner. I enjoyed listening to music, podcasts or catching up with friends and family on the phone during my long drive home. Driving was always tiring for me and I often found myself struggling to stay awake, a condition I blamed on those years of driving to and from school in a nearly comatose state. I had learned to adapt however, and would be sure to have an ample supply of crunchy ice or snacks to keep me awake.

On this particular day I was even more exhausted than usual. I tried to listen to some upbeat music, but they were only playing annoying songs. I angrily turned the radio off wondering why anyone would choose to play or even record such garbage. I turned on my most recent podcast but today the host's voice was grating on my nerves and the nuances in his communication style was more than I could take. I indignantly turned that off as well. I briefly thought of calling someone, anyone, but couldn't think of anyone I wanted to bother. After all, if they cared, why weren't they calling me? I knew my kids loved me but there was no chance I was going to interrupt their day with my misery. I had valiantly held it together throughout the day, putting on a pretty face so as not to inconvenience anyone else.

Now here I was alone with my thoughts and an hour to think them. I began to reminisce about my wedding day nine years ago. As we celebrated on the beach into the evening, it seemed as though we finally had our happy ending. What more could a girl wish for? My new husband and I walked hand in hand along the beach and all seemed well with the world. My children had all made the trip to Florida and were playfully splashing each other on the beach. My parents had even traveled to celebrate this day with me and for the first time in a long time, I sensed that they approved.

I had made the courageous decision to leave an abusive home. I had struggled to put myself through school and begin a lucrative career. I had tirelessly searched for a man worthy to stand as a fatherly example to my wounded children. I had done all I knew to do, but it wasn't enough. It didn't take me too long to realize that throwing a little dirt over the top of evil and planting a pretty flower on it does not destroy the damage that is hiding just beneath the surface. I believed I was strong. I believed I was tough. I believed I could handle anything. I believed the worst was behind me. I was so wrong. If only I could go back to those days when I foolishly believed, I would value them so much more. As I glanced up ahead, I spotted an on-coming semi barreling toward me and could feel the panic and tension rise up in my chest and throat. I was powerless over these panic attacks and once they grabbed ahold of me, I had no option other than to ride them out. I fantasized about what it would be like to cross over the center line and crash head long into that semi and concluded that it wouldn't be so bad. At least then this unbearable darkness would end.

Even Though…

Made in the USA
Monee, IL
08 December 2020